Foreword

by Aubrey Manning
Emeritus Professor of Natural History, The University of Edinburgh

Britain has always been a fertile breeding ground for naturalists, never more so than in recent years, when appreciation of the countryside has become widespread. 'Nature trails' and guides to them are now familiar items in most tourist centres, the living plants and animals are a source of delight and fascination to a public which is increasingly well-informed.

The rocks on which all this life depends have been slower to catch on. Of course, in so far as they form our 'scenery', they have always inspired pleasure and sometimes awe, but their study in detail has mostly been confined to the professionals. This book is an excellent example of how things are changing. The recent discoveries in the earth sciences have revealed, at last, how our dynamic planet 'works' and we know how closely the history of life has been interwoven with the history of the rocks – this thin crust on which we live.

When filming 'Earth Story' with the BBC I met a number of geologists and they helped me, a biologist, to begin to look at the landscape through their eyes. I became fascinated by the way that they could 'read' its history using the numerous clues which the minerals and the rock formations provide. Life itself provides some of those clues in the form of fossils. With a good guide we can easily begin to interpret how the landscape formed, the movements of plate tectonics, volcanism, the action of water, ice and now the pervasive effects of human activity in what represents the last few seconds of geological time.

The Peak District has a dramatic story to tell and Dr. Fred Broadhurst is just the guide we need. For me, this book communicates the way in which biologists and earth scientists both love the natural world. We need more and more people to share this and by understanding the way it works, come to enjoy it more and be ready to take up responsibility for its conservation. This conservation is just as essential for our own long-term survival as it is for any other living thing.

Aubrey Manning is a renowned zoologist, and was the presenter of 'Earth Story' – a highly praised BBC2 TV series which described the origins and development of life and its relationship to geological processes.

Preface to 1st Edition

It was through hill walking that I became interested in geology. National Service in the pits consolidated this interest and I went on to become a professional geologist. I hope that anyone using this book will find that *their* walks become of much greater interest than they were before. Remember that walking and geology can be done at any time of the year, not just in the summer months.

This book is for walkers in the Peak District who wish to understand more about the scenery they pass through, about the rocks, quarries, and the mines. No previous knowledge of geology is assumed. An outline of the geology of the Peak District is given at the beginning of the book but this is not essential reading before any of the walks are undertaken. An attempt has been made to keep technical terms to a minimum but, where used, they are marked by an asterisk indicating that they are included in a Glossary. Illustrations by sketches have been used, in preference to photographs, so as to emphasise features of interest.

All the walks fall within the area covered by the older, but now out of print Ordnance Survey 'Tourist Map, Peak District' at the scale of 1 inch to 1 mile. The newer 'Touring Map, Peak District and Derbyshire' from the OS covers the area, but at a scale of 1:100 000. The OS Landranger series, at a scale of 1:50 000, requires four sheets for complete coverage: Sheet 109 (Walks 10 and 11); Sheet 110 (Walks 1, 2, 3, 5, 17 and 18); Sheet 118 (Walk 13 (part) and Walk 15); and Sheet 119 (Walks 4, 6, 7, 8, 9, 12, 13 (part), 14 and 16). References to the OS 1:25 000 maps – by far the best choice for route-finding – are provided at the start of each walk.

The walks have been chosen to explain the different kinds of scenery in the Peak District, also the variety of rocks and mineral deposits to be found there. The walks are not arranged in any special order. They vary in length from about two miles (3km) to about 8¾ miles (14km) and there are two instances of a common start point for two walks – which could be done separately as short walks, or combined.

Acknowledgements

It is a pleasure to acknowledge the use I have made of the rich sources of geological information which are available for the Peak District. The geological literature is greater in amount, probably, than for any other comparable area in Britain. There are several reasons for this. First, much geological research has resulted from the economic development of the area, an important source of raw materials of great national value, such as limestone today, coal, lead and copper in the past. Secondly, because the Peak District is close to a large number of universities and other centres of learning, many professional geologists owe a significant part of their training to field work in the area. Numerous research publications have resulted. Amateur geologists, too, have published much geological research on the area. Geology is one of the few sciences where amateurs, without access to sophisticated equipment, can still be involved in research.

Major sources of information about the geology of the Peak District are the many publications of the British Geological Survey, including detailed geological maps of the area, of which I have made great use.

For much inspiration, my thanks go to geological colleagues with whom I have been involved over the years with research in the Peak District. I am also indebted to members of a number of geological societies, notably the Manchester Geological Association, and to those students from the Continuing Centre of Education at the University of Manchester, the Workers' Educational Association (WEA), and the Wilmslow Guild, who have accompanied me on many geological field trips to the Peak District, and all of whom have given me much encouragement.

Finally, but most of all, thanks go to my wife, Rosemary, not only for her constant encouragement, but also for her forbearance whilst I have been preoccupied with the preparation of this book. She has accompanied me on some of the walks and has given much-valued assistance with proof reading.

Fred Broadhurst

Dedication
This book is dedicated to my grandchildren,
Ben, Anna, Tom and Talisker
in the hope that they, too,
will come to enjoy the delights of the hills

Preface to 2nd Edition

The first Edition of *Rocky Rambles in the Peak District* was published in 2001 with revisions in 2003 and 2006. Fred Broadhurst died in 2009 but the book continued to be popular so in 2012 Sigma Press agreed to publish a new revision.

This has been done with no change to the style which makes the book so accessible to all. The maps and drawings have not been altered as the character of the book would then be lost.

Thanks are due to Paul Aplin, Peter Bennett, Cath Dyson, Lucy Frame, Barbara Kleiser, Jane Michael, Pat Orchard, John Pollard, Alison and Doug Scott, Bill Sowerbutts, Hilary Tivey and John Wadsworth for their generosity in undertaking the walks with a critical eye.

Special thanks are due to Alison and Doug Scott who have given invaluable help and support.

Family members must also be mentioned for their help with the walks and their support over the last year.

Finally, my grateful thanks to Sigma Press.

Rosemary Broadhurst

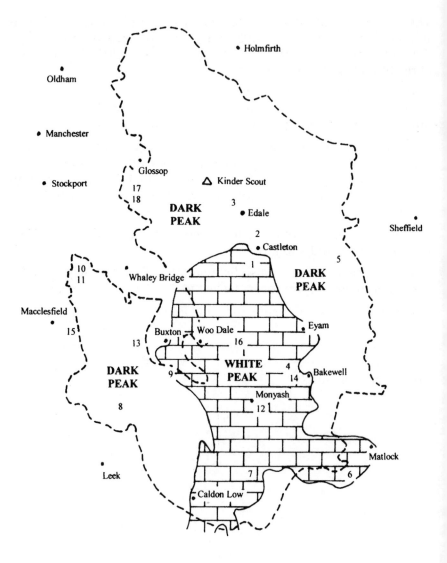

Figure 1: The boundary of the Peak District National Park (broken black line), the White Peak (brick symbol) and surrounding Dark Peak. The numbers relate to walks described in this book.

Contents

Introduction

The Walks

Introduction

About the Walks: Equipment, Maps and Access

Many of these walks cross rough terrain at some stage so strong footwear, warm clothing and adequate rainwear are strongly recommended. A whistle should be taken for emergencies! A camera (with some kind of scale that can be used in close-up photography) and binoculars are also useful. A hammer is quite unnecessary, but a penknife to test the hardness of mineral specimens (as well as to serve many other functions!) should be taken. Finally, a hand lens or magnifying glass is almost essential. In practice, the most suitable magnification is about x10. Addresses for the supply of hand lenses and other field equipment are given at the back of the book.

The route descriptions include sketch maps. These are best supported by use of the Ordnance Survey's two excellent 1:25 000 Outdoor Leisure Maps for the Peak District, Sheet OL 1 for the Dark Peak area and Sheet OL 24 for the White Peak area. A compass is always useful for indicating the general direction in which a walk should proceed ('north-west', or 'south-south-east', etc). There are several localities where a rise in the ground blocks the forward view, and here the use of a compass can avoid much frustration. No times are given for the walks, because times will vary according to the interests of the walker.

Geological maps, produced by the British Geological Survey, are available for the Peak District and details of sheet numbers are given with each walk description. The entire area is covered by geological maps at the scale of 1:50 000. Maps for some districts are available as a 'Solid and Drift' edition and show the distribution of both the rocks (the 'Solid') and the superficial deposits, such as clays and sands (the 'Drift'). Some districts are covered by two editions, one being the 'Solid and Drift', the second being either a 'Solid' (with no 'Drift' information) or a 'Solid with Drift' (with limited 'Drift' information). If in doubt, get the 'Solid with Drift'! There are also some geological 1:25 000 scale maps for areas of special geological interest. These, too, are referred to in the walk descriptions. The Geological Survey has also published an excellent Holiday Geology Map for the Peak District. A contact address and phone number are given at the back of the book.

Distances are given in miles, with a metric equivalent. Heights are given in feet with a metric equivalent. Thickness of rock strata is given in metres (to follow the practice in all scientific publications).

It has been assumed that most walkers will reach the start point of walks by car. However, it is possible to make use of public transport in the Peak District. No route details or timetables are given in this book because such details are always subject to change. However information about public transport is available from either, the Peak District Information Centre at Bakewell, telephone (01629) 813227, or the Public Transport Unit, Derbyshire County Council, Matlock, telephone (01629) 580000 or e-mail peak.connections@ peakdistrict.gov.uk or publictransport@derbyshire.gov.uk.

An Introduction to the Peak District

The Peak District lies at the southern end of the Pennines, incorporating parts of Cheshire, Greater Manchester, West Yorkshire, South Yorkshire, Derbyshire and Staffordshire. Its name derives from the Old English *peac* meaning hill. There are no peaks in terms of great mountains. The central part of the area is composed of high plateaux, which reach to just over 2,000ft (610m) on Kinder Scout, and which are cut by deep valleys. Flanking the plateau areas to west and east, respectively, there are hills.

The Peak District National Park was established in 1951, the first National Park in Great Britain. It is also the busiest National Park in terms of visitors, being surrounded by major towns and cities, with the result that about 17 million people live within some 60 miles of its boundary. Many of the entrance points to the National Park are marked by a millstone, which is the emblem of the Park, and which is one of the most distinctive of the local products from the past.

Within the National Park there are two distinct areas, see Fig. 1. One of these, the White Peak, is characterised by white limestone in rock outcrops, quarries, and in the stone of the houses and drystone walls. The plateaux of the White Peak are cut by deep and interesting valleys, the 'Dales', many of which are dry and without streams, because the drainage is underground. This is the area of caves and cave deposits. The other region is that of the Dark Peak, where the most conspicuous and toughest rock is sandstone, often coarse in grain size and referred to as 'gritstone'. This rock weathers to a brownish colour and is seen in many escarpments or 'edges', quarries, and also as building material in houses and drystone walls. If the need arises to identify location in terms of White Peak or Dark Peak, it is necessary to look only at the drystone walls; none of the material there will have been brought very far. Much of the high ground in the Dark Peak is covered by peat.

In the past and up to the present time the Peak District has been the source of raw materials of great value to the nation. Particularly important today is limestone, produced for use in the chemical industry, for agriculture and in the building industry as cement and aggregate. Fluorspar (fluorite) is also worked today. In the past lead and copper mining have been of great importance.

Outline of the Geology of the Peak District

Introduction: Minerals and Rocks

In the Peak District, as everywhere else, the essential rock-forming materials in the ground are minerals*, such as quartz*, feldspar* and calcite*. These minerals each have a particular chemical composition, or particular range of chemical compositions. Thus quartz is silicon dioxide (or silica), calcite is calcium carbonate. In addition, each kind of mineral has its own particular arrangement of atoms in the form of scaffolding. When minerals associate together, they form a rock*. Whereas most rocks are composed of several different minerals, some may be composed of only one mineral. Some of the limestones* in the Peak District, for instance, are composed of more than 99 per cent calcite.

Most of the rocks of the Peak District are layered or stratified* and even casual inspection shows them once to have been sediments of various kinds, now compacted and cemented to form rock. Where the sedimentary grains (each a particle of rock or mineral) consist of sand or silt, the resulting rock is sandstone*, or siltstone*, respectively. Some sandstones are coarse-grained, even containing pebbles, and in the past have been called 'grit'. In other cases the sedimentary material is composed of the remains of shells (usually made of the mineral calcite) or skeletons of organisms, essentially calcareous and generally light, forming limestone*. Then there are rock strata composed of what was once mud, generally dark in hue because of enclosed organic (mostly plant) matter, and now referred to as clayrock*, formerly as 'shale'. Finally, there are beds of what was once volcanic ash, now compacted to form tuff*. All of these rocks, accumulated in layers, are examples of a major group of rocks, the Sedimentary Rocks*.

In addition to the Sedimentary Rocks in the Peak District there are rocks which formed from molten rock material, or magma*, and which belong to the Igneous ('Fire') Rocks*. These Peak District rocks include a number of ancient lava flows, all composed of basalt*, a black, fine-grained, rock. A number of the minerals in basalt have a relatively high iron content and, on weathering*, the iron combines with oxygen and water to produce the familiar rust colouration on basalt outcrops. These lavas often contain gas bubbles, which may be empty, or may be filled by later mineral deposition. Masses of basalt, or its coarser-grained equivalent, dolerite*, are found associated with volcanic vents on the site of old volcanoes. The coarser grain size of dolerite results from slower cooling at depth below the surface.

The third, and last, major group of rocks comprises the Metamorphic Rocks* and includes rocks which have been altered by heat and/or pressure to develop new minerals. Such rocks are rare in the Peak District but occur locally where limestone has been baked into marble* by the heat associated with volcanic activity.

In parts of the Peak District there are many mineral deposits where the rock contains unusual assemblages of minerals, including the lead ore galena*, copper ore chalcopyrite*, together with fluorite* (or fluorspar*), calcite, and many other minerals.

The Age of the Rocks in the Peak District

The rocks of the Peak District contain many different kinds of fossils*. These are the remains and traces of animals, plants and bacteria-like forms, which were buried and preserved in ancient sediment. The fossil record as preserved elsewhere in the world indicates that fossils found at particular levels in rock strata differ from those found at other levels. A geological time scale, based on the changing pattern in the fossil record has long been established, see Fig. 2. The fossils from the Peak District rocks mostly, but not all, relate to the Carboniferous*. Note that there is a Carboniferous Period (of time) and also a Carboniferous System (of rocks). The name Carboniferous was chosen by Conybeare in 1822 to reflect the richness (in Wales) of these rocks in coal. However fossils can indicate only relative* age. They indicate that the rocks of the Peak District are older than, say, those of the Whitby area (Jurassic*), or younger than those around Wenlock Edge (Silurian*).

However, in the Carboniferous rocks of the Peak District, and elsewhere, there are volcanic rocks in which some of the minerals contain radioactive atoms. The spontaneous decay* of these atoms releases energy but also leads to the formation of new 'daughter' products. So, with time, the composition of the radioactive minerals changes, at rates that are well established. Analysis of the radioactive minerals allows their age, and therefore the date of the formation of

ERA	PERIOD, SUB PERIOD, EPOCH			AGE
CENOZOIC	Quaternary	**Holocene or Recent**		
		--10,000 years		
		Pleistocene (Glacial, Interglacial cycles, the last Glaciation, the Devensian, ending 10,000 years ago)		
		-- 2 m yrs		
	Tertiary	**Pliocene**		
		------------(date of Brassington Formation) --------------- 5 m yrs		
		Miocene		
		-- 25 m yrs		
		Oligocene		
		Eocene		
		Palaeocene		
		-- 65 m yrs		
MESOZOIC	Cretaceous			
	-- 144 m yrs			
	Jurassic			
	-- 213 m yrs			
	Triassic			
	-- 248 m yrs			
PALAEOZOIC	Permian			
	-- 286 m yrs			
	Carboniferous	**Late Carboniferous**	**Westphalian** (Coal Measures)	
			------------------------- 315 m yrs	
			Namurian (Millstone Grit)	
			-------------------------320 m yrs	
		Early Carboniferous	**Dinantian**	
	-- 360 m yrs			
	Devonian			
	-- 408 m yrs			
	Silurian			
	-- 438 m yrs			
	Ordovician			
	-- 505 m yrs			
	Cambrian			
	590 m yrs			

PRECAMBRIAN ERAS

Origin of the Earth about--- 4,600 m yrs

Figure 2. Divisions of Geological Time. Those represented in the Peak District are shown in bold. (m yrs = million years)

the enclosing rock, to be determined, in terms of years. The technique is known as radiometric dating*. The age of the Carboniferous rocks ranges from about 360 million years to about 286 million years. Such dates are remarkable when compared with the length of a human lifetime. However, when compared with the date of formation of the Earth, the Carboniferous is seen to be not so very old. The Earth is about 4,600 million years in age (as estimated by radiometric dating). If the whole of geological time could be compressed into one year, with the origin of the Earth being on 1st January, then the Carboniferous started on 3rd December and lasted for 6 days. On the same time scale, our emergence from Africa as modern man, *Homo sapiens,* occurred (approximately 100,000 years ago) about 12 minutes before midnight on New Year's Eve!

Formation of the Rocks of the Peak District

The rocks exposed in both the White and the Dark Peak are predominantly of Carboniferous age. In many places, the limestones of the White Peak can be seen to pass beneath the sandstones of the Dark Peak. This indicates that the sandstone sequences are younger than the limestones and relates to the so-called Law of Superposition* which states that in a sequence of undisturbed strata younger rocks occur above the older. Accordingly, the limestone-rich rocks of the White Peak are referred to as the Lower Carboniferous rocks, those of the Dark Peak are the Upper Carboniferous. Boreholes drilled in the Dark Peak would be expected to penetrate the Lower Carboniferous at depth.

The total thickness of the Carboniferous sediments exposed in the Peak District (though not in any one place!) reaches a maximum of about 1800m (over a mile). This could be interpreted as meaning that there was some kind of basin into which 1800m of sediment could be accommodated. However there is evidence at many levels within these rocks of deposition in shallow water. For instance, in the Lower Carboniferous, many limestones have solution surfaces which indicate weathering at times of emergence above water level. In the Upper Carboniferous, each of the numerous coal seams indicates the establishment of peat swamps. A better interpretation is that sedimentation occurred in a subsiding basin and that sedimentation kept up with the rate of subsidence. A summary of the Carboniferous succession in the Peak District is given in Fig. 3. The limestones of the Lower Carboniferous are largely composed of

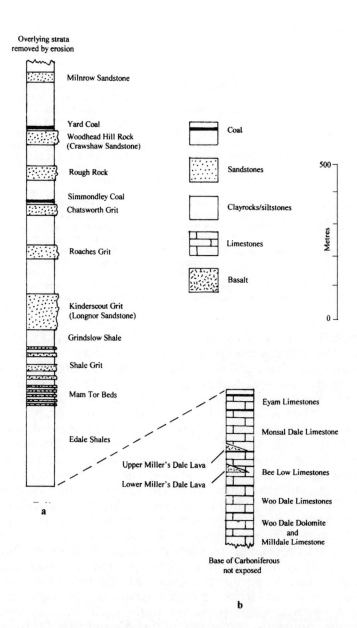

Figure 3. Generalised succession of strata present in the Peak District.
a: Upper Carboniferous; b: Lower Carboniferous

Figure 4: Some of the more common fossils to be seen in the Peak District. The bar scales indicate about 5cm or 2 inches.
a) Fossil soil or 'seatearth' with roots, now preserved as carbonaceous films. Upper Carboniferous rocks.
b) The root system Stigmaria, commonly found in the fossil soils (seatearths) associated with the swamp deposits represented in the Upper Carboniferous rocks.
c) The pith cast (infilling) of a horsetail, Calamites, a swamp plant. The ornamentation was formed by the conducting tissues in the stem. Upper Carboniferous rocks.
d) The impression of tree bark, with leaf scars, Lepidodendron, a swamp tree which reached heights of 40m. related to the modern clubmosses. Upper Carboniferous rocks.
e) The impression of tree bark, with leaf scars, Sigillaria, a swamp tree related to the modern clubmosses which reached heights of 30m. Upper Carboniferous rocks
f) The skeleton of a 'solitary' coral. Such corals were unable to cement themselves to the substrate, so with growth often toppled over and had to 'correct' their direction of growth, producing the horn shape so commonly seen.
g) The skeleton of the 'colonial' coral Lithostrotion which is very common in the Lower Carboniferous. Note the cross section which indicates that growth was regular and not influenced by seasonal growth, indicating that this coral lived in a tropical or sub-tropical environment where there were no 'summers or winters'.
h) Crinoid (or sea lily), rarely seen complete, but lengths of stem or single stem ossicles are abundant in the Lower Carboniferous Limestone.
i) and j) Productoid Brachiopods. Note that these shells are concavo-convex. Such brachiopods are abundant in the 'shelf' limestones of the Lower Carboniferous.
k) and l) Brachiopods. Note the dissimilarity of the valves. Such brachiopods are common in the 'reefs' of the Lower Carboniferous.

marine shell debris, broken up by storm action or transportation by currents. Occasionally beds of limestone are found in which much of the shell material has survived to yield fossils in an excellent state of preservation. Limestone does not compress under compaction, unlike clayrocks, so the fossils are preserved uncompressed and undistorted. The fossils include corals*, brachiopods* (a group of sea shells now much reduced in importance, but abundant during the Carboniferous), crinoids* (also known as sea lilies despite being animals and, like the brachiopods, now very rare in modern seas), and many other groups, see Fig. 4. The total assemblage is very rich.

Where growth structures are seen in the fossils, there is no evidence of seasonal growth, suggesting a life environment under tropical conditions where seasonal fluctuation is minimal. Some of these Carboniferous rocks, here and elsewhere, retain a magnetisation ('remanent' magnetism*) acquired from the Earth's magnetic field at the time they were deposited (as sediments), or extruded (as lavas). In tropical regions the magnetic field is nearly horizontal, as distinct from the high magnetic dip* in the vicinity of the Poles. The magnetism preserved in the Carboniferous rocks of this region indicates formation in near-Equatorial latitudes, a conclusion consistent with the evidence from the fossils. In fact, it appears that the Peak District in early Carboniferous times, lay just

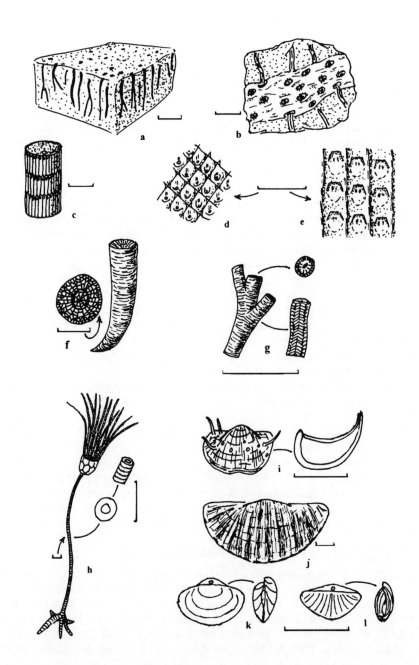

south of the Equator, but crossed that line during the late Carboniferous.

In modern tropical seas where lime-rich, potential limestone, deposits are accumulating, reefs are found. In the Carboniferous Limestone of the Peak District reef-like structures are found, but they lack the skeletal, binding framework so characteristic of modern reefs. Nevertheless, it is clear that these structures were bound (cemented) in some way, probably by bacterial activity. Where these structures formed on flat sea floors they are known as knoll reefs*. Where they formed at the margins of shelf sea areas, adjacent to deep water, they are known as apron reefs*.

The sandstones and associated rocks of the Upper Carboniferous were accumulated in extensive river channels and lagoons in a vast, subsiding, delta complex that formed across northern England. Colonisation by plants established peat swamps. Progressive deep burial under sediment converted peats into coal and also released silica to cement the sands into tough sandstones.

The volcanic (basaltic) rocks of the Peak District are restricted to the White Peak, being directly associated with the Lower Carboniferous deposits. Phases of volcanicity occurred during the time of predominantly limestone deposition. Several basalt lava flows are known and a number of volcanic vents* or pipes on the sites of original volcanoes. There are also numerous volcanic ash (tuff*) bands interbedded with the limestones.

The mineral deposits of the Peak District are varied and occur in a variety of forms. The lead ores, which are found over much of the White Peak, occur mostly in near-vertical veins (locally known as rakes*), usually a few metres in width, and which follow faults* (planes of fractured ground where displacement has occurred). Mineralisation*, by fluids ascending from below, clearly post-dated the faulting. The copper ores of the Peak District appear to be restricted to the Ecton area and occur as veins and associated massive vertical pipes. The mineral deposits supported a substantial mining industry between the late 18th and late 19th centuries.

Geological Structures in the Peak District

The most obvious geological feature of the rocks of the Peak District is probably the presence of bedding or stratification, brought about by changes in the nature of the rocks between one layer and the next. This stratification is generally crossed by breaks, or joints*, Fig. 5, which lie more or less at right angles to the bedding. There is no displacement between the opposite sides of joints, a feature which distinguishes them from faults. Jointing is best developed at the surface and generally becomes less pronounced with depth, as can be demonstrated in mines, tunnels or deep boreholes. It appears that jointing is a response to the reduction of overburden load by erosion

Figure 5: Looking upwards at the sandstone in Tegg's Nose Quarry, with stratification (bedding) which is nearly horizontal, and joints, which are nearly vertical.

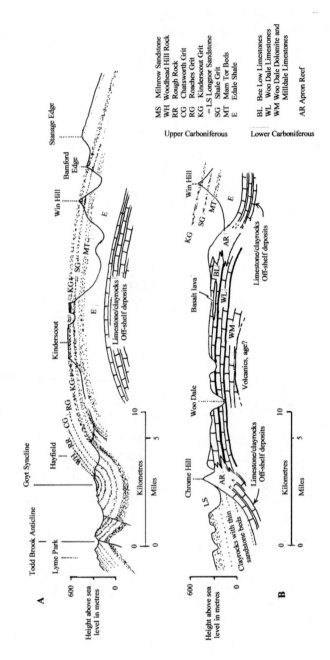

MS Milnrow Sandstone
WH Woodhead Hill Rock
RR Rough Rock
CG Chatsworth Grit
RG Roaches Grit
KG Kinderscout Grit
    = LS Longnor Sandstone
SG Shale Grit
MT Mam Tor Beds
E   Edale Shale

Upper Carboniferous

BL Bee Low Limestones
WL Woo Dale Limestones
WM Woo Dale Dolomite and
    Milldale Limestones

Lower Carboniferous

AR Apron Reef

Figure 6: Diagrammatic cross sections to show geological structures in the Peak District.
Note that the vertical scale is more than 5 times the horizontal scale.
A: Section from Lyme Park through Kinder Scout to Stanage Edge. B: Section from Chrome Hill area to Win Hill.

at the surface. As rocks are removed by erosion, the underlying beds expand by the opening up of joint systems.

Although much of the White Peak area consists of more or less horizontal limestone strata it is clear that elsewhere there has been much deformation, demonstrated by the presence of rock folds and faults. The major structure is that of a north-south trending upfold or anticline*, generally referred to as the 'Derbyshire Dome'. This structure has brought the oldest, Lower Carboniferous, rocks to the surface in the central (White Peak) area, with the Upper Carboniferous exposed on the flanks to east and west, respectively. The Upper Carboniferous in the west has been folded into a number of smaller anticlines and synclines* (downfolds). A composite west-east section across the Peak District is shown in Fig. 6.

The Peak District rocks are broken by a number of faults where there is evidence, in some places, of vertical displacement and, elsewhere, of lateral displacement. The folds and faults affect both the Lower and the Upper Carboniferous so are post-depositional in date and occurred at the end of the Carboniferous and into the following Permian*. The fold axes* are not all aligned in the same direction, so crustal shortening by compression is not an adequate explanation. It appears that movement, or jostling, of fault blocks* in the deeply buried basement are probably a major cause of the structures. The lead and copper mineralisation must be later in age than that of the faulting.

Geological History of the Peak District

1. The Basement

The oldest rocks exposed at the surface in the Peak District are limestones of early Carboniferous age. Nowhere has the pre-Carboniferous basement been exposed. However, three boreholes have penetrated the limestones. The Woo Dale Borehole, drilled near Buxton, entered volcanic rocks, of uncertain age, but possibly Precambrian* at a depth of just over 273m. The Eyam Borehole proved sedimentary rocks of Ordovician* age at a depth of just over 1800m, and the Caldon Low Borehole entered sedimentary rocks of presumed Devonian* age at about 350m.

2. The Early Carboniferous

Evidence from the Peak District, but mostly from elsewhere, suggests that a land area with irregular topography was progressively flooded by incursions of the sea during the early Carboniferous. Deposition of limestones followed. The first deposits to form are buried at a level below the present land surface, so have been seen only in boreholes. The limestones now seen at outcrop* reach a maximum thickness of about 800m. Their features suggest that the sea floor was highly varied in form, including shelf areas of shallow water, something like the Bahamas Banks of today. On the shelves isolated limestone mounds of a reef-like nature formed, the knoll reefs.

At the edges of the shelf regions there were more reef-like structures, apron-reefs, strung out in a line along the shelf edge. On the submarine slopes associated with the apron-reef limestone was accumulated, with the strata dipping towards the deeper water at angles close to the angle of rest of lime sediment. It is important to recognise this depositional dip* in these limestones and not to confuse it with tilting produced by later rock deformation. The technique for doing this is very simple and relies upon the recognition within the limestones of tell-tale 'spirit levels' which indicate the plane of the horizontal at the time of deposition. The most interesting of the 'spirit levels' are formed by partial infillings of cavities, such as are often found inside fossils, Fig. 7. These partial infills are known as geopetal ('Earth-seeking') infills*. In some cases the sea floor sloped to form a ramp between shallow water at one end and deep water at the other. In deeper, off-shelf, regions the deposition of lime sediment was accompanied by the deposition of much mud, which, with its associated organic content, made the limestones dark in hue. Within these deeper water areas, localised 'highs' permitted the development of knoll-reefs.

The varied topography of the early Carboniferous sea floor is attributed to an overall stretching of the crust, which was relieved by

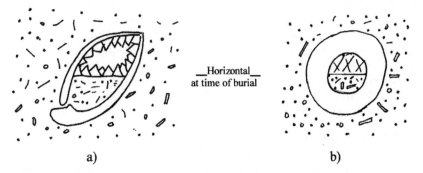

Figure 7: Partial infilling of cavities (= geopetal infills) inside rocks or fossils as a means of determining the horizontal at the time of sediment deposition. a) in a brachiopod, b) in a crinoid.

the development of faults and rotation of fault blocks. Such a process would be associated with many earthquakes. The stretching of the crust would also produce crustal thinning (in the same way that a piece of elastic is thinned when stretched) and would account for the subsidence that provided the space for so much Carboniferous sediment. Such deformation of crustal rocks is now linked to the concept of Plate Tectonics* whereby segments (Plates) of the Earth's crust can be moved, rotated, stretched or compressed by the flow (really 'creep') of mantle* currents below the crust, in the same manner that rafts are carried by currents in the sea.

The nature of the Lower Carboniferous volcanicity in the Peak District fits well with the concept of crustal tension in the underlying crust. The composition of basalt is such that derivation from the mantle is highly probable. Furthermore, a volcanic vent at Calton Hill, near Buxton, is noted for the occurrence there, in the basaltic rocks, of inclusions of lherzolite, a rock with the composition of mantle. It appears that pieces of the mantle were brought up to the surface during the course of volcanic eruptions. Fissures, to allow the ascent of molten rock* from the mantle to the surface, are most likely to develop when the crust is in tension.

3. The Late Carboniferous

At the close of the early Carboniferous, it appears that a fall in sea level, or a rise in land level, occurred. Exposed areas above sea level were subjected to erosion, but in the deeper water areas sedimentation continued without a break from the Lower to the Upper Carboniferous. In such areas the rock types such as clayrocks and impure limestones are to be found across both sides of the boundary separating the Lower from the Upper Carboniferous. By international agreement, one fossil-rich band with characteristic fossils is defined as the boundary.

Progressive flooding brought a return of the sea across the Peak District and a resumption of sediment deposition, but now by mud, to form the Edale Shales, see Fig. 3. The arrival of mud at this time ended the prolific life that had been so important in forming the limestones of the Lower Carboniferous. Today these clayrocks are undergoing removal by erosion to reveal the buried, irregular, surface of the limestone beneath. Remarkably, in parts of the Castleton district this surface coincides with bedding in the limestone, so is a resurrected sea floor topography.

The Edale Shales are the first indication of a delta in the north. The succession of sedimentary rocks above the Edale Shales record the progressive extension of this delta into the Peak District and the development of vast braided* river systems which brought in the coarse-grained sands, now the sandstones ('gritstones') so characteristic of the Upper Carboniferous in the Peak District. The delta top was frequently colonised by vegetation and extensive peat swamps formed, which later became the coal seams of the area. On a number of occasions the sea level rose and flooded the delta top, bringing about the deposition of clayrocks containing marine fossils. Such marine bands* (between less than a metre to several metres in thickness) probably owe their origin to sea level rises caused by melting of a southern hemisphere ice cap which existed at this time. The fossils found in the marine bands include coiled shells known as goniatites*, the precursors to the ammonites of the Jurassic and Cretaceous Periods. The goniatites were undergoing rapid evolution during the late Carboniferous and successive marine bands can be identified by their particular goniatite content.

The thickness of the Upper Carboniferous rocks in places in the Peak District is well over 2,000m, much of it formed at, or above, sea level. The subsidence which started during the early Carboniferous continued, but faulting and block rotation were now replaced by even subsidence. The environment of deposition of these rocks, on the evidence of their magnetism and the absence of growth rings in the fossil plant material, was equatorial. This is the time when the Peak District sat on the Equator. It has taken about 300 million years to move the Peak District (courtesy of Plate Tectonics) to where it is today.

Deformation at the end of the Carboniferous

Following the deposition of the Carboniferous sediments conditions in the crust below the Peak District changed from tensional to compressional. The rocks were deformed by folding and faulting. Subsidence stopped and uplift ensued. These events in the Peak District reflected major events elsewhere, events which involved collision between continental masses and the final unification of all the Earth's continental crust into a single supercontinent known as Pangaea*.

The gentle fold of the Peak Dome, the folds seen in the western part of the area, and the faulting, all date from this time. The deformation was partly caused by compression, partly by jostling of fault blocks in the basement.

Post-Carboniferous History

At some stage after deformation of the Carboniferous mineralisation began. Hot aqueous (hydrothermal*) solutions rich in dissolved salts are thought to have been responsible. The circulation of hot ground water at depth is thought to have taken up metals in solution from the surrounding rocks and, by convection, risen towards the surface to deposit the metals, generally as sulphides, in fault fracture planes or other cavities. Although such a process was probably slow, it had the enormity of geological time in which to take place. The copper mineralisation in the Ecton district is quite unlike most of the mineralisation elsewhere in the Peak District and the implication is that the hydrothermal solutions there had a source quite distinct from that of the lead mineralisation.

Apart from the mineral deposits, there is little material younger than the Carboniferous preserved in the Peak District and it is necessary to look elsewhere for evidence. In the areas around the Peak District, there are outcrops of strata which, at one time, probably extended over the Peak District before their removal by erosion. These rocks include Permo-Triassic* sediments, often referred to as the New Red Sandstones*, because of their predominantly red colouration. Over much of Britain these rocks have many features indicating deposition in an arid, desert-like, environment, appropriate for a formation where there is palaeomagnetic evidence for deposition at a latitude close to 30°N, the latitude of the Sahara Desert (a warning here! It is known that magnetic polarity reverses* from time to time, so the New Red Sandstones *might* have been formed at about 30°S. However the simplest interpretation is 30°N). The Permo-Triassic rocks over parts of the Peak District may have included the Magnesian Limestone*, a marine formation well known from the north-east of England. This formation might be the source of magnesium-rich brines which brought about the dolomitisation* in the Wirksworth area. However, it is also possible that the process of dolomitisation may be related to the mineralisation of the district. Such a situation merits further research.

Another possible consequence of burial by the Permo-Triassic rocks is that the Carboniferous surface, immediately beneath the Permo-Triassic cover, was weathered under arid conditions, prior to burial by desert sediments on a land surface. In localities (away from the Peak District) where the contact between the Carboniferous and the New Red Sandstone is exposed, the Carboniferous rocks below the contact are generally reddened*, due to such weathering. In various parts of the Peak District, as on the Roaches, for instance, reddened rocks suggest that the New Red Sandstone cover was once not far above.

Following the Permo-Triassic the rock record elsewhere in Britain indicates a time of generally rising sea levels, through the Jurassic* and Cretaceous* Periods. It is unknown to what extent the Peak District would be flooded during this time. However, sea levels by the close of the Cretaceous were exceptionally high, globally, and coincided with deposition of the Chalk* (a soft limestone). It seems quite likely that the Chalk was deposited across the Peak District. If so, it has all now been removed by erosion. The end of the Cretaceous, about 65 million years ago, was marked by a major asteroid impact in the Yucatan Peninsula (Mexico) and also a major outburst of volcanicity in the Deccan (India), the two events coinciding with a major extinction event* (notably involving the dinosaurs). At this time there was a (related?) major fall in global sea levels and it is likely that the Peak District became part of the land again.

The post-Cretaceous (Tertiary* and Quaternary*, see Fig. 2) history of the Peak District, as elsewhere in Britain, has involved uplift, associated with the opening of the North Atlantic Ocean. During the late Miocene*-early Pliocene*, about 5 million years ago, river-lain sediments were deposited over much of the southern part of the Peak District. Little is left of these sediments because of subsequent erosion, but remnants are preserved in subsidence hollows in the limestone of the White Peak, in the southern part of the Peak District. The deposits are known as the Brassington Formation*. They have been worked as a source of quartz-rich refractory* sand.

During the course of the Tertiary, there was global cooling which became more marked as time progressed. The Arctic Ice cap came into being about 2.5 million years ago. Its size fluctuated in response to cyclic variations (known as Milankovitch Cycles*) in the amount of solar energy received by the Earth, due to changes in the shape of the Earth's orbit around the Sun, and changes in the inclination and direction of the Earth's rotational axis. The process of northerly movement (Plate Tectonics) has brought Britain within range of these ice caps when at their maximum extent and several glaciations have occurred. These glaciations commenced about 2 million years ago and ended, with the last, or Devensian* Glaciation, about 10,000 years ago. The time since the last glaciation is known as the Holocene* or Recent. There is little doubt that there will be more glaciations in the future! The intervals between glaciations were known as interglacials*, when temperatures were similar to, or even higher than, those of today.

Glacial and interglacial periods each lasted for approximately one hundred thousand years or thereabouts.

In the Peak District, deposits formed during the Pleistocene are widespread and comprise a large proportion of the superficial deposits (the so-called 'Drift'*) which rest on the 'Solid'* rocks below. Important among the Pleistocene sediments is boulder clay*, or till, which was deposited by ice, the boulders often including rock types which indicate their provenance (usually the Lake District or Southern Scotland). Melt water deposits of sand and gravel are also found. Most Pleistocene deposits relate to the last, or Devensian, Glaciation. The Peak District was close to the southern limit of the ice during the Devensian and many areas were not glaciated.

The post-Glacial or Holocene history of the Peak District is notable in that our own species appears on the scene in the capacity of a geological agent. The forests were largely cleared by about 7,000 years ago, and with the advent of the Industrial Revolution major impacts on the landscape of the Peak District have been made due to the extraction of raw materials. Such activity continues on a grand scale, but has been joined in more recent years by the new industry of tourism, promoting conflicts over land use.

Walk 1: Castleton – Cave Dale – Pin Dale

Limestones, Lava and Lead

Start of Walk: Main car park, Castleton. (SK 149 830)

Maps:
Topographical: 1:25 000 OS Explorer OL1, The Peak District, Dark Peak Area.
Geological: British Geological Survey 1:25 000 Sheet SK 18 and Part of SK17, Edale and Castleton. 1:50 000 Sheet 99, Chapel-en-le-Frith (Solid Edition and Drift Edition)

Distance: 4¾ miles (7.5km)

Refreshments: Pubs, cafés in Castleton.

From the car park and visitor centre walk towards the centre of Castleton, locating Castle Street which leads to a point directly beneath the Norman Peveril Castle, which is perched on the hill above the village. The National Park Information Centre in the car park is well worth a visit. At the castle end of Castle Street turn into the square (Market Place), then right at Cave Dale Cottage into Bar Gate and Cave Dale (signed). A few metres into Bar Gate, by the information boards and before entering the narrow entrance into Cave Dale, note the small abandoned quarry working, behind the gardens, on the right. It will be seen that the dip of the limestones* here is about 30°, and roughly parallel to the slope of the adjacent hillside. Elsewhere the presence of fossil 'spirit levels', in the form of geopetal infills*(Fig. 7) indicates that this dip is depositional, meaning that the limestones accumulated on a slope of about 30°. It appears that these rocks, referred to as apron-reef*, were accumulated as flank deposits below the edge of a shallow shelf sea to the south. Continue through the narrow entrance to Cave Dale and note that the limestones on both sides of the Dale exhibit approximately the same direction and amount of dip.

Walk up the Dale along the northern-most part of the "Limestone Way" which extends south to Matlock (26 miles) and Rocester in Dovedale (46 miles). Enjoy the good views of Peveril Castle perched on the crags above, in a superb defensive position. Further up, the Dale curves to the left and the dip of the limestones is seen to be slackening, eventually to become practically horizontal once the 'shelf' area is reached. Walk into the curve, then turn left into a conspicuous gully (locality 1, Fig. 8) where there is a mineral vein or, rather, a complex of veins occupied mainly by calcite*, but also by galena*, the latter best seen on the left margin of the complex. Many of the cavities in this vein are natural, others are man-made. The

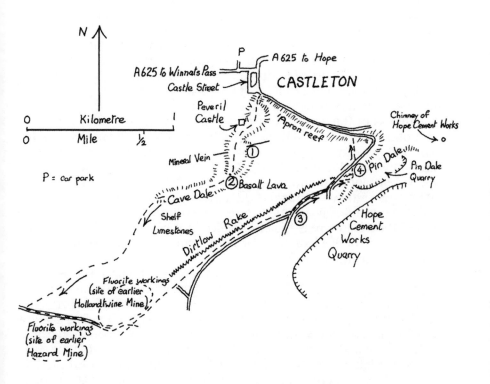

Figure 8: Sketch map of the Castleton - Cave Dale area

mineral vein is continued on the opposite side of Cave Dale and has been explored by the many trial pits seen.

Continue up Cave Dale, noting that the limestone beds are now nearly horizontal. These limestones, formed on the floor of a shelf sea, are known as the Bee Low limestones (see Fig. 3). Pass a cave entrance protected by a metal grill, then reach a gate beyond which there are outcrops of basalt* lava (locality 2, Fig. 8), readily identified on account of its dark brown colouration. Fresh basalt is virtually black, but on weathering the relatively high iron content of the rock leads to the development of iron oxides and hydroxides (familiar to us all as rust) which are brown in colour. To the left of the path the first outcrops of lava include a basalt column*, of the type associated with the Giant's Causeway in Antrim, and indicative of slow cooling and consolidation on a land surface. This observation is of considerable interest when it is borne in mind that the limestones, seen both above and below the lava are marine in character. Clearly the area was raised above sea level (or sea level had dropped) at the time of the volcanicity. Search will reveal basalt with gas bubbles (vesicular* lava), some of which have been occupied by minerals such as calcite. Whilst at this locality note that there is a change in the gradient of the valley floor here. The gradient of Cave Dale is gentle down to the level of the lava outcrops but is much steeper below the lava. The toughness of the lava is controlling the form of the valley profile.

Continue up Cave Dale, noting the terracettes* on the valley sides. The Dale becomes progressively shallower higher up. Outcrops of limestone reveal that some beds (with few layers of clay 'impurity') are more resistant to weathering than others (where clay layers are more abundant). A dew pond is passed, a reminder of the problem of water shortage for animals on limestone at times during the year. Towards the top of the Dale there is much evidence of lead working. Finally a stile, constructed of sandstone* slabs but capped by limestone rich in crinoid* remains, leads to a road.

Turn left (eastwards) and note the tips of the disused Hazard Mine on the right. Ahead at the site of the disused Hollandwine Mine, an information board describes the geology, mining history and landscape restoration of one of the best-known lead veins, Dirtlow Rake. (The remaining quarry at the southern end of Dirtlow Rake is on private land and access is only by prior arrangement by phoning 0143 622351 (daytime only)). These tips and veins were reworked to recover fluorite before they were landscaped to farmland and to open up a view of the Mam Tor – Whin Hill sandstone ridge to the north. The mineral fluorite was of no interest to the original lead miners but is valuable today in the manufacture of a variety of products including hydrochlorofluorocarbons for use as refrigerants, aerosol propellants, etc. (and replacing the chlorofluorocarbons which led to ozone damage in the atmosphere). The road runs alongside the workings and is flanked in places by large boulders, which should be inspected carefully. Some are mineralised, some contain fossils. Many changes are taking place along Dirtlow Rake and opportunities should be exploited to look at new dumps or disturbed ground in search of minerals and fossils. As the road is followed alongside Dirtlow Rake workings, the Hope Cement Works will be seen ahead.

The limestone needed by the cement works is worked in the large quarry which comes into view to the right (east). The clay material needed by the cement works is extracted at the Folly, seen to the left of the works chimney. This clay material comes from the Upper

Carboniferous Mam Tor Beds (see Fig. 3). Two road junctions are met, close together. In both cases, turn left, in the direction of the cement works. At the first junction (locality 3, Fig. 8) look over the walls to the right. The large blocks of rock seen in the field consist of silicified limestone (chert*) and have remained here whilst solution of the underlying limestone has taken place. At the second junction, which lies close to the head of Pin Dale, note the large block of stone on the right-hand side of the junction. This block is of limestone but with much silica* replacement (as chert).

Continue along the road leading towards Castleton. Shortly the road crosses Dirtlow Rake. On approaching the line of the rake, take the footpath which leads off from the right-hand side of the road heading in the direction of Pin Dale (locality 4, Fig. 8). This path descends a short distance to cross workings in Dirtlow Rake, then climbs back to rejoin the road. During the summer months this is a good locality to see the Vernal Sandwort or Leadwort, *Minuartia verna* (Fig. 9) which is tolerant of lead. Good views can be had of both Dirtlow Rake and Pin Dale. Note that the bedding of the limestones at the top of Pin Dale is nearly horizontal (Bee Low 'shelf' limestone), but that it dips down in the apron-reef towards the north-east, in the vicinity of the cement works. Deep water formerly extended to the north and the east.

Continue along the road beyond Dirtlow Rake and just after the road sign (indicating road gradient, single-track road, and need for low gear!) cross through the stile on the left side of the road. There is an indistinct path which heads roughly northwards (aim for Lose Hill) down a very steep slope to a stile at the road below. The steep hillside here is developed on the apron-reef, as seen in the entrance to Cave Dale. At the road, turn left into Castleton and the car parks. Note the limestone walls of the houses, the sandstone lintels and doorframes (sandstone is more easily shaped than limestone), and sandstone flags on the roofs.

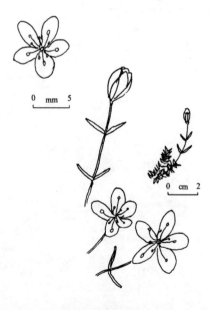

Figure 9: The Vernal Sandwort or Leadwort, *Minuartia verna*

Walk 2: Castleton – Lose Hill – Mam Tor

Ridge, Landslip and a Resurrected Sea Floor

Start of Walk: Main car park, Castleton (SK149 830)

Maps:

    Topographical: 1:25 000 OS Explorer Map:OL1, The Peak District, Dark
Peak Area.
    Geological: British Geological Survey 1:25 000 Sheet SK 18 and Part of
SK17, Edale and Castleton. 1:50 000 Sheet 99, Chapel-en-le-Frith (Solid
Edition and Drift Edition)

Distance: 7¾ miles (12.5km)

Refreshments: Pubs and cafés in Castleton

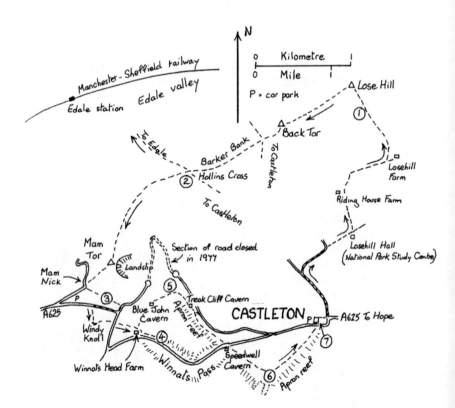

Figure 10: Sketch map of the Castleton - Mam Tor area

Start from the north-east corner of the car park (by the stream) and walk along a path to a road junction. Note the limestone* construction of the house walls but use of sandstone* (as flags) in the roofs. In some cases, flags have been replaced by slate. Turn left at the junction, away from the village, following signs for Hollins Cross and Edale. Cross a stream, pass a cemetery and then a private playing field intended for the use of permanent residents of Castleton. Take the right fork at the next road junction and walk past the training and conference centre. The blocks in the limestone walls around here are rich in fossils. At a sharp left bend in the road, continue straight on along a footpath signed for Losehill. Pass Losehill Hall on the right, then in a few metres turn left up a path signed for Lose Hill. This path follows the line of an incised* stream, heading directly for Lose Hill ahead. Pass Riding House Farm on the left. The route, well signed for Lose Hill, curves round towards Losehill Farm (in a group of trees), but before reaching the farm, heads up the slopes towards the summit of Lose Hill. Note that wall construction is now in sandstone, which has replaced the limestone of the walls lower down. Occasional outcrops reveal siltstones* and sandstones. Once above the level of Losehill Farm (locality 1, Fig. 10) the views over the surrounding country become impressive. The landslip scar of Mam Tor, is seen away to the

Figure 11: Mam Tor and the Winnats from the slopes of Lose Hill

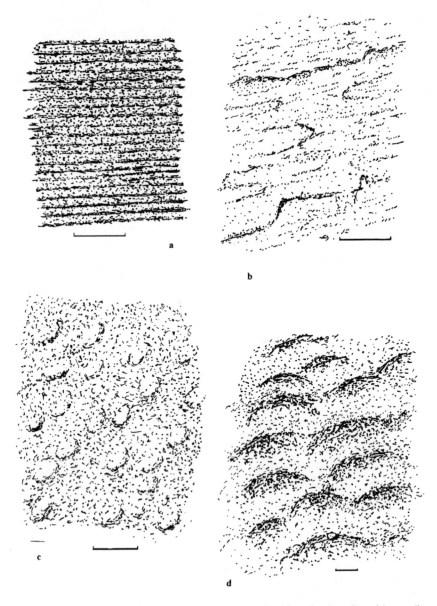

Figure 12: Features of flagstone surfaces: a) saw marks; b) parting lineation; c) 'mussel' impressions; d) fossil ripple marks. For explanations, see Glossary of Terms and text. Scale bar = 5cm

west. Note that the Upper Carboniferous strata of Mam Tor, if continued into space to the left (south) would overlie the Lower Carboniferous limestone hills around Castleton – see Fig. 11. There is a good view of the Winnats, the spectacular gorge in the limestone, to the left of Mam Tor, which is visited later on this walk. To the south is the large limestone quarry, which provides stone for the Hope Cement Works immediately to its left. The broad Hope Valley below is floored by the relatively soft Edale Shales (see Fig. 3) of the Upper Carboniferous. This shale*, or clayrock*, sits directly on the limestone of the Lower Carboniferous below.

Proceed to the summit of Lose Hill. Sandstone flags have been laid here in the interests of footpath conservation. These flags are mostly derived from old mills and other industrial premises now demolished. On the surfaces of these flags there are interesting geological features, such as fossil ripple marks*, parting lineation*, and saw marks* – see Fig. 12.

From the summit of Lose Hill, there is an excellent all-round view. To the north and north-west is the Edale valley. This valley has a U-shaped* profile (see Fig. 13) suggesting a glacial origin. However there are no glacial deposits known from this valley and the U-shaped profile is the result of landslides, over a long period of time, which have caused the valley sides to slip into the valley floor. The floor and lower sides of the valley are underlain by the same Edale Shales formation as that which underlies the Hope valley. This rock formation is weak and in sloping ground is subject to the development of landslips. The Mam Tor landslip, already seen, is an example. To the east, across the valley of the River Noe, is the summit of Win Hill, capped by sandstone, the Kinderscout Grit. Win Hill summit is composed of the last remnant of what was once a continuous sheet of sandstone extending from Kinder Scout, above the level of Lose Hill, to areas well beyond Win Hill. Such a remnant is known as an outlier*. The view from Lose Hill also takes in the magnificent ridge between Lose Hill and Mam Tor – see Fig. 14. That ridge is the next stage of the walk.

Continue westwards to the summit of Back Tor, partly over sandstone flags. The sandstone and siltstone* strata in the face and summit area belong to the Shale Grit, a formation which, elsewhere, lies below the Kinderscout Grit – see Fig. 3. Below Back Tor, in the Edale valley is an excellent example of a landslip, with its hummocky surface. Leave Back Tor and walk down the steep path to the west, at the same time looking out for specimens of mudflake conglomerate*, easy to spot because of the pronounced contrast between the dark

Figure 13: The U-form of the Edale valley, seen from Lose Hill.

'mudflake' pebbles and the light sandstone matrix. Once down the steep slope be sure to look back for the good view of the rock face of Back Tor. In a few metres a col is reached which is crossed by a path linking Castleton with Edale. Carry on towards Mam Tor over Barker Bank. In the vicinity of the next col, at Hollins Cross (where another path from Castleton to Edale crosses the ridge) there are good views of Mam Tor. Note the landslip scar itself, the upper part of which is occupied by the Mam Tor Beds, another rock succession of alternating thin sandstones and siltstones – see Fig. 3. At the base of the landslip scar, the topmost beds of the dark Edale Shale can be seen. Below the landslip scar, the landslip debris is seen as a glacier-like mass.

In the vicinity of Hollins Cross (locality 2, Fig. 10) there are more sandstone flags for footpath conservation, together with rock outcrops, including sandstones, mudflake conglomerates and siltstones. To the south, the hillsides around Castleton are composed of apron-reef* limestone where the dip of the strata is roughly parallel with the slope of the hillsides themselves. These dips can be shown to be original features of the limestone because of the presence of natural 'spirit levels' in the form of geopetal infills* (Fig. 7). Beyond Castleton, to the south and the west, the limestone strata are more or

Figure 14: The ridge between Lose Hill and Mam Tor, looking towards Mam Tor.

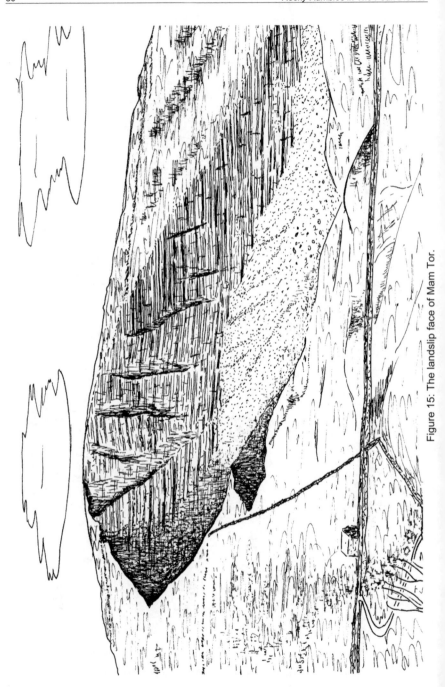

Figure 15: The landslip face of Mam Tor.

less level and accumulated on a flat shelf in shallow water. So the view from Hollins Cross is that of a resurrected Carboniferous sea floor, with a shelf sea to the south ending at 30° slopes, around Castleton, and passing into deep water under the Hope valley and areas to the north. This resurrected seafloor topography is being progressively exposed as the Upper Carboniferous sediments are removed by erosion. A few million years ago the limestones would still have been buried by the Upper Carboniferous. A few million years into the future and erosion will have destroyed so much of the limestone that the story will be lost. Lucky is the rambler of today!

Continue to the summit of Mam Tor, noting outcrops of sandstone and siltstone in the path. Note that the sandstones are different from most sandstones of this area in that they are dark because of included mud and organic material. These sandstones were formed not by river deposition, but by deposition from underwater avalanches of sediment on a delta front. Each avalanche generated a 'turbidity current' (a mix of sediment and water moving down the delta front by gravity) leading to the deposition in front of the delta of a 'turbidite' deposit. These turbidites will be seen to advantage shortly in the face of Mam Tor. Close to the summit of Mam Tor the path is again protected with sandstone flags, some with magnificent fossil ripples, others with mussel* impressions. Note the Iron Age defence ditches around the summit. Enjoy the good views from the summit.

Walk, with care, down from the summit to see the top of the landslip face – see Fig. 15. The Mam Tor Beds are well seen at this type locality and consist of the thin muddy sandstones, each a turbidite, examples of which have already been seen in the path, interbedded with siltstones and clayrocks. The silt-clay beds represent the quiet periods in between the arrival of turbidity currents. Below the landslip scar is the great mass of landslip debris and the remains of the road that was closed in 1977 because of the high cost of its maintenance over such unstable ground. Return to the summit area and the path. Follow the path westwards down to the col at Mam Nick, noting the geological features of the sandstone flags along the pathway. Note also the presence of mica in many of the sandstone rocks alongside the path. Close to the junction with the road at Mam Nick, there is a boulder to the right of the path with a fossil plant. The cutting on the far side (western) of the road at Mam Nick reveals an exposure of the Mam Tor Beds. This exposure is difficult to approach but can be appreciated at a distance. Note that the sandstones (turbidites) each have a sharp base but an indistinct top where they 'merge' into the overlying siltstone/clayrock. Each turbidity current arrived suddenly, sweeping and even eroding the surface of mud below, prior to dumping its load of muddy sand. The finest grains transported by the flow would settle last, and would be similar in size to the particles that normally accumulated here.

From the road return to the path and walk southwards along the line of the flags to the gate, then turn left, following the sign for Blue John Cavern, in the direction of the cement works. Do not follow the path to Cavedale and Peak Forest. A disused quarry seen on the other side of the road below is to be visited later. Walk over the nearby tips (locality 3, Fig. 10) from the Odin Mine, to see specimens of calcite* and galena*. Weathered galena becomes grey, so should be scraped with a penknife blade, or other instrument, to reveal its bright metallic lustre. At appropriate times of the year, the Vernal Sandwort, or Leadwort, *Minuartia verna*, will be seen – see Fig. 9. This plant is tolerant to lead in the soil. The lead workings here were reached by shafts sunk through the Upper Carboniferous rocks to the Odin Vein in the limestones below. Note that the mineralisation did not continue from the limestones into the overlying Upper Carboniferous. Odin Vein, like many of the lead veins, lies along a fault. Fault movement in limestone produced much fracturing, and created space for mineralisation. But the Upper Carboniferous rocks here are composed of the clay-rich Edale Shales which were self-sealing after fault movement. Upward flow of mineralising solutions would therefore be stopped close to the limestone/clayrock boundary, the clays acting as a kind of damp-proof course. From the mine tips carry on to the road below, crossing an area of peat from which water issues, with floating films of iron oxides and hydroxides (providing an opportunity for the 'oil test'*). Turn right on the minor road below, to join the A625, then walk up to Windy Knoll Quarry.

Take the entrance road to the quarry and head for the quarry face directly ahead. The top part of this face is covered by a black mass of bituminous material, which is worth close inspection. In places it can be handled and can be drawn out into strings, like elastic. But, beware! Such an experiment will leave the hands dirty and smelly! This is a natural deposit and is the residue left behind after the evaporation of oil. It is known as elaterite*. It is probable that there was once a significant accumulation of oil here, but erosion has unroofed its covering seal and the oil has now been lost. The presence here, and elsewhere, of such deposits has encouraged exploration for hydrocarbons in the district, but without success so far. The rock face exposed at lower levels, beneath the bitumen deposit, is interesting because 'fossilised' fissures in the limestone are filled with limestone

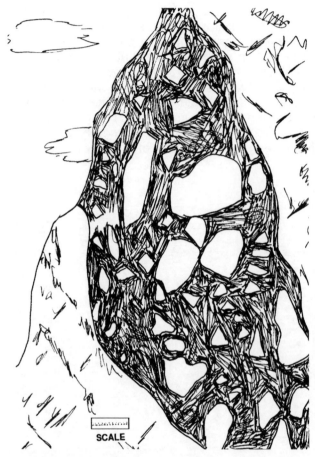

Figure 16: 'Neptunean' dyke, Windy Knoll. Scale bar = 10cm

fragments set in a dark matrix - see Fig. 16. It appears that the fissures (often referred to as 'Neptunian Dykes'*) were developed in the limestone by solution at a time when the limestones were raised above sea level (or the sea level had fallen!). The fissures were subsequently filled by debris, and finally buried beneath the marine mud deposits of the Edale Shales. The Edale Shales would have provided the ideal seal for the oil deposit.

When Windy Knoll Quarry was being worked, a fissure revealed a collection of mammalian bones which appeared to have been washed in during the late Pleistocene*. These bones include the remains of reindeer, grizzly bear, bison and other animals.

Walk eastwards, past a cave entrance, and cross the (A625) road. The stile on the far side of the road contains crinoid and other fossil remains, nicely polished by walkers' boots. Head for Winnats Head Farm ahead (and signed). Keep to the left of the farm buildings, and continue in the direction of the Winnats Pass (signed). Walk into the Winnats with the road and its boundary wall to the right. Walk the few metres necessary (locality 4, Fig. 10) to get a good view down the gorge

– see Fig. 17. The Winnats Pass represents a gorge originally formed soon after deposition of the limestones, but before the deposition of the Edale Shales of the Upper Carboniferous. The gorge appears to have been formed by marine currents, possibly tidal, flowing between the shallow 'shelf' region of limestone deposition and the deeper 'basin'. After formation, the gorge was buried beneath a thick deposit of marine muds, now represented by the Edale Shales. These Shales have now been removed by erosion from the gorge, thus resurrecting a part of the Carboniferous sea floor. Subsequent minor modification to the form of the gorge has taken place. A remarkable situation.

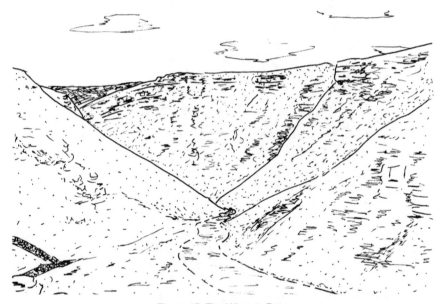

Figure 17: The Winnats Pass

Return to Winnats Head Farm and take the path signed for Blue John Cavern. As the cave is approached, there are good views of the Mam Tor landslip. The cavern takes its name from the variety of fluorite* called Blue John*. The cause of the banding is not fully understood, but appears to develop where fluorite has been exposed to radiation. The source of the radiation is the Edale Shale, which contains traces of radioactive material. The process involves the knocking out of some of the fluorine atoms from the atomic structure of the fluorite and migration of the 'freed' calcium atoms to produce the colour bands that distinguish Blue John. This material is worked into ornaments, vases, etc. However, it retains the properties of fluorite so is rather soft and subject to easy breakage along the mineral cleavages*. Deposits of Blue John may be seen in this and other caves in the district. Probably the best material is to be seen at Treak Cliff Cavern, passed shortly in this walk. Blue John ornaments are readily available for sale at many of the shops in Castleton.

At Blue John Cavern ignore the path leading to the road on the left but continue eastwards, through a stile on the path leading to Treak Cliff Cavern. The walk continues, with Win Hill ahead. After the next gate, the path leads to the right of a steep gully (locality 5, Fig. 10). Exposures of limestone on the opposite (left) side of the gully reveal poorly developed bedding, which dips to the east at about the same angle as the hillside. Fossil 'spirit levels' or geopetal infills* (see Fig. 7) occur here, but access is difficult and such features are more easily seen elsewhere, notably on Walk 12 in Lathkill Dale. These geopetal infills indicate that the dip is 'original', meaning that these limestones are part of the apron reef* and were deposited on a slope of about 30°, the angle of rest for carbonate sediments on the seafloor. Deeper water lay downslope to the east. It is known that the types of fossil found here change in a down-dip direction, presumably in response to the changing water depths when the animals were alive. The hillside around Treak Cliff Cavern coincides, more or less, with bedding planes of the apron reef beneath. Beyond Speedwell and towards Castleton, the hillside, and the bedding planes, swing round eastwards. All this ground is part of the resurrected Carboniferous sea floor. How many other walkers will appreciate that?

At Treak Cliff Cavern (worth a visit to see not only excellent cave formations such as stalactites* and stalagmites*, but also stunning deposits of Blue John) start down the path leading to the road, then turn off right on a rough path leading to the Speedwell Cavern and pass more exposures of the 'apron reef'. Continue to the buildings at Speedwell, at the foot of the Winnats. There is another cave here, Speedwell Cavern, open to visitors and involving an underground boat trip. Enjoy another view of the spectacular Winnats Pass. Exposures, which are difficult of access, around the foot of the Winnats, contain numerous rolled and rounded fossil shells. It is probable that this material was originally transported from the 'shelf' down the Winnats gorge and dumped at its base. The walls around Speedwell are largely made of this shelly material but better examples will be seen in Castleton.

Continue along the path south-eastwards from Speedwell. There are many small old quarry workings here, mostly in the shelly limestone just described. Shortly this path makes a left turn (at locality 6, Fig. 10), to follow the apron reef as it swings round towards Castleton. Just before this left turn, leave the path and walk about 10m or so up the slope to the south-east. A mound here is composed of basaltic material, with a number of small exposures. Note the typical brown weathering of the basalt. On inspection the material is much broken (or brecciated*) and laboratory examination has shown that originally there was much basaltic glass developed here. This material appears to be basalt lava that entered water, partly exploded to produce fragments and partly chilled instantly to produce glass. It is likely that this material is the seaward equivalent of the subaerial basalt lava seen on Walk 1 into Cave Dale. If this is correct it means that the Cave Dale lava flowed across the shelf at a time when the shelf was above sea level, came to the edge of the shelf, then flowed down the (apron reef) slope into the sea somewhere in this vicinity. Prior to the work that established this material to be of submarine origin, this locality had been interpreted as possibly a volcanic vent and the name 'Speedwell Vent' appears in the older literature.

Continue along the path back to Castleton, noting that the hillside to the right is the continuation of the apron reef. Back in the village head for the car park, but, at the main road, turn right for a few metres to the Bull's Head (locality 7, Fig. 10). The building blocks here provide splendid examples of the shelly limestone that can be seen around Speedwell. Return to the car park.

Walk 3: Edale – Kinder Scout

Sandstone Scenery, Wind Sculptures

Start of Walk: Car park, near Edale Station (SK 124 853).

Maps:
> Topographical: 1:25 000 OS Explorer Map: OL1, The Peak District, Dark Peak Area.
> Geological: British Geological Survey 1:25 000 Sheet SK 18 and Part of SK17, Edale and Castleton. 1:50 000 Sheet 99, Chapel-en-le-Frith (Solid Edition and Drift Edition)

Distance: 7¾ miles (12.5km)

Refreshments: Pubs and cafés in Edale

Leave the car park via the exit (close to the toilets) and turn right to follow the road under the railway bridge and into Edale village. The Peak National Park Visitor Centre (the Moorlands Centre), passed on the right, is well worth a visit. Note the sandstone* construction of many of the buildings in Edale, some with sandstone flags on the roofs (e.g. the Old Nag's Head). The slate seen on other roofs was brought here by the railway. Continue along the road northwards from the village, to take the Grindsbrook Clough path leading off right (well signed) from the road. The word 'Clough' means 'Ravine'. The path crosses Grinds Brook, then bears left (locality 1, Fig. 18), in an upstream direction. The path has been protected against erosion by sandstone flags, mostly derived from the demolition of former mills. These flags exhibit a number of features of interest. Some show the saw marks* produced when the stones were cut by frame saws. Others have fossil ripple marks* in various states of erosion, mussel impressions* (both positives and negatives) and parting lineation* (particularly impressive towards the end of the flagged path as it approaches the wood) – see Fig. 12. Enter the wood, then cross a tributary of Grinds Brook by a footbridge to carry on up the main valley. There are impressive views up the deeply incised valley. Waterfalls indicate the outcrops of tough bands of sandstone. The edge of the Kinder Scout plateau contains many outcrops of sandstone, known as the Kinderscout Grit (where 'grit' refers to coarse-grained sandstone) – see Fig. 3. Fallen blocks of this material are to be seen at many points along the path. Note the conspicuous pebbles of quartz* within it. Ascending the path, a rockfall can be identified ahead, where a landslide has occurred below Upper Tor.

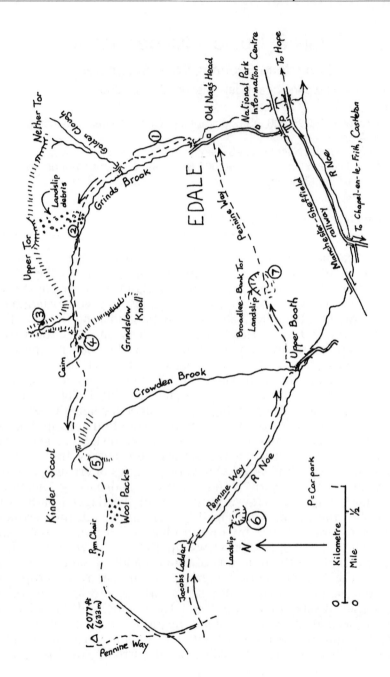

Figure 18: Sketch map of the Edale - Kinder Scout area

Before reaching this landslip debris the view towards Grinds Brook, reveals extensive outcrops of clayrocks*, dark because of included organic (plant) debris. Such clayrocks occur between the sandstone beds which form the waterfalls and rapids seen in the stream. This part of the succession is known as the Shale Grit (see Fig. 3).

On reaching the landslip debris, look for springs emerging from beneath the peat. The water develops a surface film, of iron oxides and iron hydroxides, which resembles a film of oil. Apply the 'oil test'*. Organic matter (in this case peat) and iron are generally associated together. Various alternative paths appear at this point to cross the blocks in the landslip debris. It is best to aim high. Where all the paths reunite above the debris (locality 2, Fig. 18), look for loose blocks, immediately alongside the path on the right, with fossil plant remains, also some blocks of sandstone containing pellets and flakes of clayrock, material known as mudflake conglomerate*. In places, the 'mudflakes' have been eroded out of the host rock to leave characteristic holes and depressions.

The path shortly crosses the stream to continue along its western bank (the true right bank). In this vicinity many of the sandstones are dark in colour and are mixtures of sand, silt and clay-sized grains with organic (mostly plant) matter. These rocks are known as 'turbidites' formed by deposition from underwater avalanches or 'turbidity currents'. The depositional setting here is one of a delta front where material sliding towards deeper water (to the south in this case) started the formation of turbidity currents. A few metres above the point where the path crosses the stream, a splendid outcrop of the Grindslow Shales (Fig. 3) will be seen above a ponded section of Grinds Brook. These rocks are dominated by dark (organic-rich) clayrocks* and siltstones*, with thin grey siltstone bands. Close inspection shows that some of these sediments are involved in slump* folds. Loose blocks reveal bedding planes rich in mica* flakes. The path continues to the point where Grinds Brook flows off the Kinder Scout plateau. The last section of the path is steep, across fallen blocks of the Kinderscout Grit, with massive outcrops of the 'grit' to be seen all around.

From the top of the path, turn right (north) along the edge of the plateau to walk a short distance to the head of a major tributary to Grinds Brook (locality 3, Fig. 18). There is a striking exposure here of the Kinderscout Grit with the stream flowing over bedding planes. Return to the top of the Grinds Brook path and walk to the cairn (locality 4, Fig.18). Look to the south-east to identify the Anvil Stone (Fig. 19) – a block of Kinderscout Grit shaped by sandblasting caused

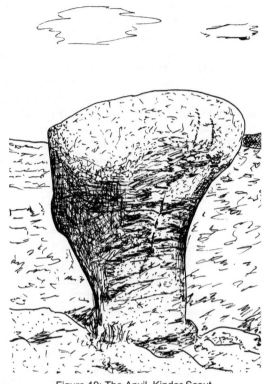

Figure 19: The Anvil, Kinder Scout.

by wind acting on the abundant supply of sand released by rock weathering. Part way between the cairn and the Anvil Stone, outcrops of the Kinderscout Grit reveal that, in places, much decay of the sandstone has occurred. The stone most subject to decay has a cement of calcite*, calcium carbonate, readily attacked by the acid waters associated with the peat present everywhere here. The more resistant sandstone is cemented by silica*, silicon dioxide, not readily attacked by the peat acids. In the vicinity of the Anvil Stone, small patches of calcite-cemented sandstone have been completely removed by erosion – Fig. 20. All these calcite-cemented patches of sandstone are referred to as carbonate concretions* (because of the calcite, calcium carbonate, cement) and were probably formed by the inclusion of plant debris in the original sandy deposit. Bacterial decay changed the chemistry of the formation water and caused the precipitation of the calcite cement. The calcite often contains iron as an 'impurity' so the process of calcite (or, better, 'ferroan calcite') weathering often leads to red staining because of the presence of iron oxides and hydroxides.

From the Anvil Stone a flagged (erosion control) pathway will be seen a few metres away to the west. Walk along this pathway noting fossil ripple marks. In a few metres, another flagged path comes in from the right. At and around this junction look closely at the flags. Fossil plant material is preserved here, also mussel impressions – see

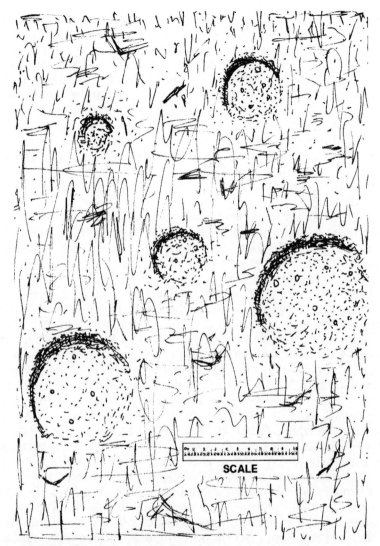

Figure 20: Solution cavities on the site of carbonate concretions. Scale bar = 10cm

Fig. 12c. Continue along the flagged path towards the west, towards the top of Crowden Brook, noting the development of peat across the Kinder Scout plateau. This peat dates back about 7,000 years and started to form after deforestation by man. Where silica-cemented sandstone is in contact with the peat the rock is often white, due to the progressive breakdown of feldspar* grains in the rock to the (white) clay mineral kaolinite*. Where the sandstone contains large grains of feldspar, these become conspicuous because of this development of white kaolinite. If the feldspar is abundant then its destruction in this way produces a 'spongy' rock with numerous holes and cavities. Sandstones with a calcareous cement are rapidly broken down into sand by the acidity of the peat water. The sand released by these weathering processes lies around everywhere and is available for natural sandblasting whenever there are high winds. In the vicinity of the peat much iron-staining will be seen in places. Iron and organic matter are generally associated, and here weathering of the iron component is producing the rust colours of iron oxides and hydroxides.

As Crowden Brook is reached, Crowden Tower lies ahead (locality 5, Fig. 18). It consists of sandstone outcrops, with plant fossils in places, and where the joint* systems have been widened by the action of sandblasting to produce a number of blocks, some of which have rotated to some degree. The action of the wind on these blocks has produced striking sculptures, worthy of a place in any art gallery. The western-most 'sculpture' is quite remarkable. Continue west-south-west to the Woolpacks (Fig. 21) – more blocks sculpted by the wind. The sculptures continue to Pym's Chair but then the track begins a gradual descent to meet the Pennine Way at the Swine's Back. There are good views of the Edale Valley from here. Note its U-shaped profile (see Fig. 13) which is the result of its collapsed sides produced through many landslides over long periods of time (and not from former glaciation, the usual reason for U-shaped valleys). The route is now well-signed and leads down to Jacob's Ladder, so called because steps were made here for the use of packhorses by Jacob Marshall. There are two notices here, one relating to the peat deposits on the hills, the other to path renovation and conservation.

Beyond Jacob's Ladder a splendid example of a landslip is to be seen on the right-hand side of the valley (locality 6, Fig. 18). The incision* of the stream valleys is most remarkable around here. Before reaching Upper Booth, note the black clayrocks of the Edale Shale which occupy the floor of the Edale Valley. These rocks are mechanically very weak and are responsible for the landslips hereabouts. Looking up at the hills around note the terrace-like feature produced by the outcrop of the more easily-weathered and eroded Grindslow Shale. In Upper Booth turn left at the telephone kiosk, following signs to Edale. Beyond Upper Booth the footpath threads its way across a landslip (locality 7, Fig. 18) below

Figure 21: The Woolpacks, produced by sand blasting, Kinder Scout.

Broadlee-Bank Tor; the landslip face (in the Shale Grit) and the masses of slipped material are most impressive. From the highest point of the footpath on this landslip there is an excellent view of the (U-shaped) Edale Valley, the landslips on Rushup Edge and Mam Tor, opposite. Once back in Edale turn right for the station and car park.

Walk 4: Monsal Dale

Landslips and Fossils

Start of Walk: Car park, at Monsal Head (SK 184 715).

Maps:
  Topographical: 1:25 000OS Explorer Map:OL24, The Peak District, White Peak Area.
  Geological: British Geological Survey1:25 000 Sheet SK 17, Miller's Dale.
  1:50 000 British Geological Sheet 111, Buxton (Solid and Drift Edition)

Distance: 8¾ miles (14km)

Refreshments: Pub, café at Monsal Head

Figure 22: Sketch map of the Monsal Dale - Litton Mill area

Leave the car park, pass between the buildings to reach the viewpoint over Monsal Dale and the viaduct of the abandoned railway line, now the Monsal Trail. Two tracks lead off down into Monsal Dale from here. Take the route indicated as leading to 'Ashford and Monsal Dale' and 'Ashford'. Continue through a gate. The path descends evenly at first, steepening in parts as it approaches the river and the sound of the weir can be heard. A rough path can be seen to lead off to the left through the bushes at this point. The start of the path is about 100 metres before a second gate at the bottom of the descent. Take this path leading steeply uphill and very soon the massive blocks of limestone* which form Hob's House (locality 1, Fig. 22) appear. These blocks are large land-slipped masses, their walls formed by fracture along the joints* in the limestone. Cross the remnants of a limestone wall and walk up towards the left of the slipped blocks to enter the ground separating the blocks from the main cliff. One of the blocks on the left has a leaning tower on its summit. Enter the cleft to the right of this block – see Fig. 23. At the base of the cleft, on the right-hand side, will be seen the Hob's House Coral Band, about half a metre in thickness.

The Hob's House Coral Band can be followed through the cleft. The limestone matrix is dark, because of included clay and organic material and it is also well-jointed*. These limestones are known as the Monsal Dale Limestones, of which there is a dark, 'muddy' type, as here, and also a 'pure' limestone with very low clay content. These two types of limestone, are referred to as different facies*. The corals generally stand proud of the limestone surface (by up to several millimetres in some cases) because they have been partly replaced by silica*. Silica is virtually insoluble in rainwater, unlike the surrounding limestone. Differential solution is responsible for the effect seen. There are two main types of coral here. One is a branching coral, *Lithostrotion* (see Fig. 4g), with branches about a centimetre or less in width. This coral is often seen in cross-section, when growth features can be seen, suggesting that growth was even and not controlled by seasonal variations – see Fig. 4g. This situation would be expected in equatorial latitudes and there are a number of features in rocks of this age, such as their magnetic properties, which indicate deposition in tropical locations. The Peak District lay close to the Equator in Carboniferous times, some 300 million years ago! The other coral, *Dibunophyllum* (see Fig. 4f), is a solitary coral, reaching several centimetres in diameter. The corals are found lying on their sides, even upside down, and many are damaged. This suggests that they have undergone transportation before burial. Associated with

Figure 23: Hob's House, a landslip feature

the Hob's House Coral Band are limestones rich in brachiopods*, which also show evidence of transportation.

Masses of silica, known as chert*, also occur and form bands and nodules – see Fig. 34. It is clear that the chert has replaced limestone as well as fossils. Replacement of the fossils by silica is, in many cases, only partial. The question arises as to the source of the silica. Chert is common in the Peak District. In some places it appears to be related to nearby volcanic rocks, elsewhere the relationship appears to be with the mineral veins and in some places the proximity of overlying silica-rich rocks of the Upper Carboniferous rocks suggests that these rocks might be the source. Chert has been worked in the Peak District as an abrasive, used in the manufacture of high quality porcelain ware.

Walk through the cleft and continue round the towers, across scree (specimens of corals and brachiopods to be seen). Retrace your steps to return to the path leading down to the weir and continue through the gate at the end. Follow the footpath leading downstream, and cross the river by the footbridge. Note that the trees at low levels along the valley side are all large and healthy, those higher up somewhat less vigorous, the difference relating, presumably, to the availability of water through the year. The path continues, crossing mounds of scree in places. Eventually, as the sound of traffic on the A6 ahead becomes noticeable, a signpost appears, indicating the direction of 'Brushfield Hough'. Take the Brushfield path. A steep climb is involved here, with an outcrop of weathered basalt* lava to be seen in a dry channel to the right of the path a short way up. At the top of the slope the path curves to the right to Brushfield Hough. Many of the walls in this area are packed with brachiopod shells, many replaced by silica. There are good views of Monsal Dale below. Follow the yellow markers through the buildings of Brushfield Hough. Some of the walls of the buildings have been rendered at some stage but the rendering has largely detached to reveal building stones of a shelly limestone beneath. Beyond Brushfield Hough (locality 2, Fig. 22) the path lies in a lane, flanked by limestone walls extremely rich in brachiopods, many of them silicified. There is coral material, too. Much of the brachiopod material appears to have undergone transportation and damage prior to burial.

At the end of the lane, the main track bears to the left (north-westwards) across an open field. However, take the footpath that leads across the field in a north-easterly direction. At the junction follow the sign to Upper Dale. This pathway soon provides good views over Monsal Dale and the Hobs House landslip on the far side. Workings in the Putwell Hill (lead) Vein appear to the right of the track and run parallel with it. The walls along the track are rich in fossils. There are also small limestone outcrops along the roadside. These outcrops contain examples of brachiopods, the best of which are to be seen in an outcrop close to the point where the Putwell Hill Vein passes beneath the road (and where the road makes its closest approach to a power line on the left (locality 3, Fig 22). Access to the worked ground is easy here and specimens of galena* can be seen, also (at appropriate times of the year) examples of *Minuartia verna*, the Vernal Sandwort or Leadwort (Fig. 9), the plant which is a good indicator of lead in the soil. The walls alongside the road at this point are partly constructed of material from the lead vein and include masses of calcite* and some galena. There is light grey chert also in this wall and it is possible on casual inspection to confuse the chert with the calcite. The penknife test is called for (calcite is easily scratched, but not the chert). At this point, return to the start of the detour in the vicinity of Brushfield Hough, then continue westwards, following the footpath sign for Brushfield.

A disused limestone quarry on the left exposes white, pure, Monsal Dale Limestone (in contrast to the dark 'facies', seen earlier). Continue to the hamlet of Brushfield, then take the right fork (the left fork being signed for Taddington). Follow the sign for Priestcliffe. The track continues to the right of a farm (Top Farm) and past a copse of trees on the left. At the far end of the copse, a line of trees on the right-hand side of the road marks the location of workings along a lead vein. Lead workings such as these were generally fenced to keep out animals, thereby giving vegetation, such as trees, a chance to grow. The path now lies along the edge of the remarkably straight High Dale, seen down below to the left. Beyond, there is a good view of Taddington to the south-east.

Continue along the straight road, then through a protracted Z-bend, to a metal gate. Pass through the gate, down into a hollow and in a few metres reach a footpath sign on the right of the road. Take the path indicated, heading towards the north-east, with a wall to its right. This path, is soon joined by another, to continue across old lead workings (locality 4, Fig. 22) to level ground before commencing the steep descent into Miller's Dale. There are good views of both Miller's Dale and Tideswell Dale. On the descent into Miller's Dale, watch for a wire fence along the left-hand side of the path. On the far side of this fence is a limestone wall with fine examples of silicified corals. The path eventually reaches a bridge over the course of the abandoned railway line. Turn right along the track bed of the railway for a few metres, then follow the instruction to take a track off to the left, leading to a footbridge over the River Wye and into Litton Mill. At the start of this approach to the bridge there are steps cut into limestone, with large brachiopods exposed.

Once in Litton Mill turn right and follow the signs to Cressbrook. Pass through the imposing entrance gate to the site of the mill, which opened in 1782 and had a dreadful record of bad working conditions and long hours. Follow the path across the former mill-race from the mill and take the path alongside the river. This stretch of the Wye is known as Water-cum-Jolly Dale, which is as delightful as its name suggests. Note the horizontal bedding of the limestones here, bedding planes being picked out by thin bands of clay material. At Cressbrook the path reaches, and crosses, a weir. On the far side of the weir, the path divides. Take the right-hand branch, which crosses the Wye and leads back, over limestone scree, to the course of the old railway line. The limestone fragments in the scree belong to the dark 'facies' of the Monsal Dale Limestone. This darkness is best appreciated when pieces of the rock are broken. Exposed surfaces develop a light grey skin during the weathering process, perhaps by precipitation of lime drawn to the surface in solution.

On reaching the line of the abandoned railway examine the rocks in the vicinity of the tunnel portal here (locality 5, Fig. 22). Thinly bedded dark limestones alternate with clay bands. In particular, note the presence of chert bands and nodules which stand proud of the surface, being less soluble in rain water than the surrounding limestone. Walk along the railway track towards Monsal Head. The route approaches the old Monsal Head Station (still with its platform intact, note the use of sandstone here, with its non-slip surfaces, rather than limestone). Rock exposures seen through the bushes on the right-hand side of the track reveal horizontal strata of the impure limestone. At the former station there is a plaque with information concerning not only the railway but also the lead mining operation associated with the lead vein to be seen in the cutting 100 metres to the east (the next stop, locality 6, Fig. 22). At these workings, the Putwell Hill Vein is seen again. Most of the mineral seen here is calcite. Note that the limestone beds just beyond the workings, to the east, are disturbed, with high angles of dip, indicating movements of the fault along which the Putwell Hill Vein was emplaced.

Continuing towards Monsal Head the dip in the limestones progressively decreases until it is practically horizontal again. Note the presence of the clay partings and the bodies of chert which appear in the walls of the cuttings. There are also shell bands here, in places silicified. Look out for rather strange horizontal markings on the joint surfaces here. It would appear that before the excavation of the cuttings the joint system was frequently filled with water, up to the levels indicated. Eventually the viaduct at Monsal Head is reached. At the far end of the viaduct there is the west portal of the recently opened Monsal Head Tunnel, adjacent to which is a track leading up to Monsal Head and the car park.

Walk 5: Millstone Edge – Stanage Edge

Millstones and Concretions

Start of Walk: Surprise View Car park, Millstone Edge (SK 252 801)

NB The Pay and Display machine in the car park will not take cash, it only takes cards.

Maps:
> Topographical: 1:25 000 OS Explorer Map: OL1, The Peak District, Dark Peak Area.
> Geological: British Geological Survey 1:50 000 Sheet 99, Chapel-en-le-Frith (Solid Edition and Drift Edition)

Distance: 6½ miles (10km)

Refreshments: Pubs and cafés in Hathersage

Leave the car park by the path at its western end and continue to a stone wall in the vicinity of a seat, dedicated to 'Tommy Buxton', at the superb viewpoint known as Surprise View, over the Derwent valley. To the north-west the railway runs along the valley past Hathersage and on towards Edale. The Lose Hill – Mam Tor ridge can be seen, also Kinder Scout. The view to the left (south) down the Derwent valley is towards Chatsworth with Froggatt Edge a prominent feature. The wall by the seat is made of blocks of sandstone*, some quite coarse-grained with pebbles of quartz*.

Cross the wall at a point just to the right of the seat, where there is a kind of stile, and follow the path on the far side down to a quarry access road. Turn right on this road, walk about 40m then turn right again, down a short access path into a small disused quarry (locality 1, Fig. 24). At the end of this path, before entering the quarry itself, examine the bedding planes on the large fallen blocks in front. Some of the bedding planes reveal a mass of plant stems, in the form of a log jam. Then enter the tiny quarry and on its northern face look for the impressions of plant stems – Fig. 25. Return to the access road and turn right.

Walk for about 200m passing much spoil and a great variety of vegetation. A large quarry appears on the right (locality 2, Fig. 24). Do not be surprised to find rock-climbers practising their skills here. The sandstone is the Chatsworth Grit – see Fig. 3. In the south-eastern corner of this quarry, a rough path provides a relatively easy route from the floor to the top of the quarry. This path will be useful shortly. The features of the quarry faces include cross-stratification* – see Fig. 26. Jointing* is also

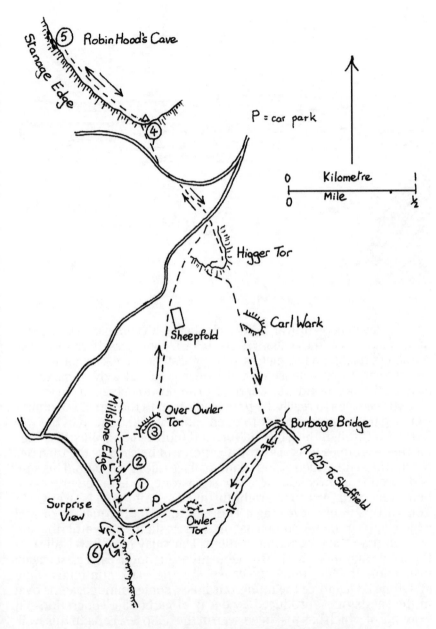

Figure 24: Sketch map of the Millstone Edge - Stanage Edge area

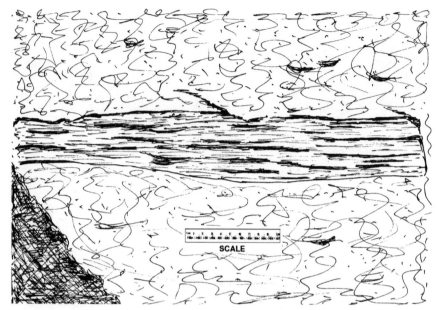

Figure 25: Fossil wood preserved as an impression, Millstone Edge. Scale bar = 10cm

well displayed here, providing rock-climbers with suitable crevices. Most of the flat faces in these quarries are, in fact, joint faces. Walk further up the access road for a few metres, past a millstone, to reach another short access road to an extension of the quarry face already seen. At this location the face includes an impressive carbonate concretion* – Fig. 27.

Retrace steps to reach the path leading up to the top of the quarry. Here a gate (an access point to open country) will be seen in the wire fence. Go through the gate and turn left (north) along Millstone Edge. Further examples of cross-stratification will be seen in the quarries. Notice the sand, which is abundant in places along the path. This sand is derived from breakdown of the sandstone, so is in the process of being recycled. Over to the right the highest point seen is Over Owler Tor with its impressive crags. Tors* are upstanding masses of rock which appear to be somewhat more resistant to weathering and erosion than the rocks around them. They may have fewer joints in them, or they may be better cemented, or both. Each case needs inspection to determine its cause. As the walk continues along Millstone Edge notice the numerous holes, some rounded, some oval, in the sandstones, produced by decay of carbonate concretions, an example of which has just been seen in the quarries. Later in this walk, evidence relating to their origin will be seen.

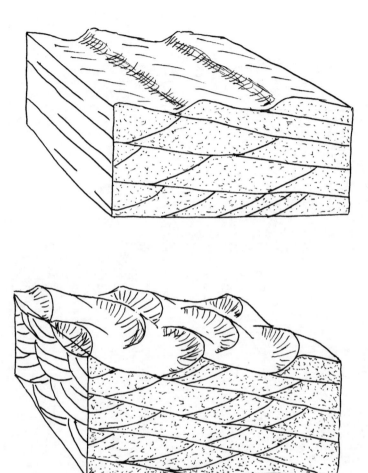

Figure 26: Cross-stratification (large scale) and cross-lamination (small scale) produced by migration of sand banks (large scale) and ripples (small scale). Current flow right to left.

Walk to the point where the wire fence takes an abrupt turn. There is a good view from here. Notice Stanage Edge to the north on the skyline, also Higger Tor, the flat-topped hill to the north-east. Walk to Over Owler Tor (locality 3, Fig. 24) and enjoy the features of the Chatsworth Grit outcrop there. Note the control exerted by the joints in the rock.

Figure 27: Carbonate concretion in sandstone, Millstone Edge. Solution of the calcite cement in the concretion is releasing sand grains which are then removed by wind.

Features of the bedding, including cross-stratification, are well seen on some of the joint faces. The wind has produced some interesting natural sculptures by differential erosion of layers of differing toughness. Carl Wark, an outcrop of sandstone with great archaeological significance is to be seen to the north-east and will be visited later in the walk. Over Owler Tor is a good point from which to note the general concordance of summit levels, suggesting that the present scenery results from erosion into what was once an elevated plateau.

Leave Over Owler Tor from a point to the north-east of the highest point. In and around this area there are sandstones associated with mudflake conglomerates*, where the rock contains numerous hollows and depressions formerly occupied by pebbles of clay or silt and which have now been removed by erosion. There are millstones here, too, and in places roughouts of millstones, suggesting that at least some of these stones were shaped from masses of rock already exposed at the surface. The path eventually reaches a sheepfold, which should be passed on the left. Beyond the sheepfold, the path heads towards Higger Tor with its sandstone (Chatsworth Grit) cap. This mass of sandstone has been isolated from the adjacent outcrops by erosion, so is an example of an outlier*. It will be appreciated, from the appearance of the crags, that the sandstone differs in toughness from place to place. Cross-stratification is to be seen here. Head for the gap between Higger Tor and the road to the left (west), then make for the point where a path from Higger Tor reaches the road at a footpath sign. Here, cross the road, then follow the path across the moor towards Stanage Edge. This path meets a minor road. Turn left on this road for a few metres, then branch off to the right on the path leading towards the triangulation point on Stanage Edge. Just before reaching the rocks of the Edge a path branches off to the right heading directly for a point (locality 4, Fig. 24) beneath the triangulation point.

This path leads to an interesting, and much photographed, group of millstones – see Fig. 28. In the rock face behind the millstones, there is a splendid exposure of part of a channel that was first cut into sand, then later infilled by sand. Return to the main track and walk up to the triangulation point. Note the distinction between the steep scarp* slope and the shallow dip* slope of the sandstone (Chatsworth Grit) here. The sandstone dips to the east at about 5°. The sandstone itself is coarse-grained and contains pebbles of quartz. It contains holes left by the removal (after solution of the carbonate cement) of concretions – see Fig. 20. Note the joint systems here, many widened by the action of wind erosion. The triangulation point is a good viewpoint.

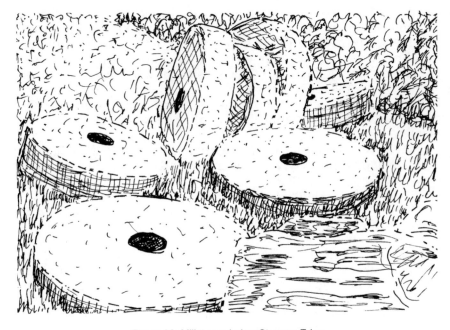

Figure 28: Millstones below Stanage Edge

From the triangulation point, walk north-westwards along Stanage Edge. Cross-stratification is to be seen, also more carbonate concretions. At Robin Hood's Cave (locality 5, Fig. 24) a number of carbonate concretions have coalesced and their dissolution has produced the cave-like structure – see Fig. 29. Entry into these caves reveals the presence of an abundance of fossil wood. The association of such wood and carbonate concretions is common. This suggests that the concretions owe their origin, in some way, to the presence of the wood. It is probable that (bacterial) decay of the wood in the original sand brought about a change in the chemistry of the formation water, a change that favoured the precipitation, locally, of a carbonate cement. A short distance beyond Robin Hood's Cave there are more plant remains, on the top surface of the sandstone at the cliff edge.

Retrace steps to the road below Higger Tor. From the road, follow the track leading up Higger Tor. On the summit area, more carbonate concretion solution holes are to be seen. There is peat up here, too, and the sandstone in close contact with the peat tends to turn white, due to the breakdown of feldspar grains in the sandstone by the

Figure 29: Robin Hood's Cave, Stanage Edge. Formed by an amalgamation of carbonate concretions now undergoing weathering.

action of the acid peat water, to (white) kaolin clay. The Chatsworth Grit here is generally rich in quartz pebbles, as it was on Stanage Edge. From the southern edge of Higger Tor there is a good view of Carl Wark below, to the south, the next stop, and of the track leading to it. However, finding the start of this track from among the rocks at the southern tip of Higger Tor is not easy. Walk along the south-western edge of Higger Tor until an easy way down is found. A path from here links up with the route to Carl Wark.

Carl Wark is the site of an Iron Age fort, with a substantial stone wall built on its most vulnerable, south-west side. There is an explanatory notice here. Be sure to examine the site of the original entrance. Head from Carl Wark south to Burbage Bridge, along any of several tracks. The main A625 road is met at Burbage Bridge. Turn left here (eastwards) for a few metres, walk round the road bend, over the bridge, then cross the road to pass through a gate and into a wood. Bear right at a fork to walk alongside the stream. Cross a footbridge and continue along the right bank of the stream. Watch out for a boulder in the stream with a striking plant fossil! This boulder is about 100m upstream from a weir. Features such as abandoned river meanders and river terraces should be noted. The path reaches a second footbridge over the river. At this point, turn away from the river and head towards the west along any of the numerous pathways hereabouts. Owler Tor eventually comes into view and should be passed on its left. Familiar features, such as cross-stratification, should be noted. The car park then comes into view.

Walk up to the gate leading to the road and car park. However, do not pass through the gate, but turn left to follow the path parallel with the road. Shortly a junction of paths is reached. Continue ahead to the west, through a stile, then at Surprise View descend the slope, curving to the right into an abandoned quarry area. Keeping to the right, continue the descent to meet a quarry access road at the bottom of the workings. Turn left, downslope. Along this road is a remarkable collection of millstones. Continue beyond the millstones to a large wooden post. From here, turn left to walk back up through the quarry to regain the path above and return to the car park.

Walk 6: Wirksworth

National Stone Centre and Dolomite

Start of Walk: Car park at National Stone Centre (SK 287 552).

Maps:

Topographical: 1:25 000 OS Explorer Map:OL24, The Peak District, White Peak Area.

Geological: British Geological Survey 1:50 000 Sheets, 111 Buxton (Solid and Drift Edition), 112 Chesterfield (Solid and Drift Edition)

Distance: 8 miles (13km)

Refreshments: Café at the National Stone Centre

From the car park walk down beneath the bridge of the old Cromford and High Peak railway (and now the High Peak Trail) to the 'Discovery Centre', where there is a rock, mineral and book shop, refreshments, and a 'Story of Stone' exhibition (open 10am – 5pm in the summer, 10am – 4pm in the winter). Leaflets are available at the Centre, including one with a trail plan and drawings of fossils seen in the limestones around the Centre. There are numbered signs at the localities referred to on the plan. To the west of the Centre there are opportunities for gem panning and stone carving and the large limestone blocks in this area contain a variety of fossils. There are also rock sculptures to see. To the north there is a flight of steps constructed from rocks sourced from throughout the UK. These are in the form of a geological column arranged in age sequence, from Precambrian at the base to Palaeogene at the top. There is a notice describing the rock types used, their ages and source locations. On the eastern side of the building there is a mine shaft, covered by a grill, but allowing inspection of the shaft below (trail locality 2). Further to the east of the Centre (at trail locality 4) there are well bedded, pure, limestones with a range of fossils including crinoids*, brachiopods* and corals. Follow the path south-eastwards and into the cul-de-sac occupied by trail locality 5 where there is view of a quarry wall with its features explained by a nearby notice. Continue southwards to trail locality 6 with another explanatory notice and drawings. On the vertical fault plane note the vein of galena* associated with calcite*, fluorite* and barite*. Some of the best galena is located very close to the notice. The bedding planes opposite contain splendid examples of large crinoid stems, or 'sea lilies' – see Fig. 31. Notice the direction of the dip* of the crinoidal limestone here. These beds are dipping off the top of a knoll reef* to be seen again, shortly, at trail locality 9.

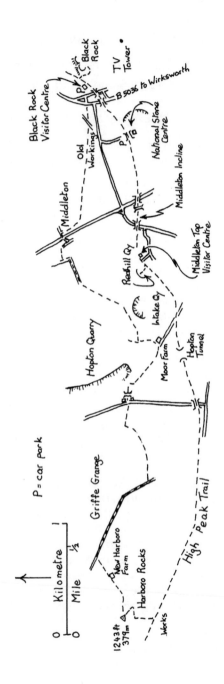

Figure 30: Sketch map of the Wirksworth area

Figure 31: Crinoid stems at the National Stone Centre, Middleton. Scale bar = 10cm.

Continue along the path to trail locality 8 where there are examples of stone walls constructed of different materials including sandstone*, limestone*, basalt* (dark green, fine-grained), dolerite* (dark green, coarse-grained, with laths of feldspar* grains), granite* (light colour, coarse-grained) and slate*. The slate is green in colour, exhibits sedimentary banding and shows good rock cleavage*, a natural plane of parting which does not coincide with the plane of the bedding. Continue to trail locality 9 where there is another explanatory diagram showing what a Carboniferous knoll reef would have looked like at the time of its formation. The limestone exposed behind and to the right of the notice is a small knoll reef but its structure is difficult to appreciate from this viewpoint. A better viewpoint of the 'reef' and its associated limestones can be reached by walking up the path directly above trail locality 4. The view from here is shown in Fig. 32. Proceed to trail locality 10 where there is a viewpoint overlooking the South East quarry. Rocks on the quarry floor are almost horizontal but those on the top edges dip quite steeply, flanking reef and slumped limestone material. Return to the car park, noting the limekiln (trail locality 3) on the right as soon as the path emerges from under the old railway bridge.

Figure 32: A Carboniferous knoll reef, National Stone Centre, Middleton.

From the car park walk to the High Peak Trail, on the course of the old railway, in the vicinity of the Rolls-Royce locomotive. Turn right, westwards. There are views from here over the old quarries and an impression gained of the amount of stone that has been extracted. Continue to the Middleton Bottom Wheel pit, formerly part of the winding gear for moving trains up and down the Middleton Incline. As the Incline is ascended it passes over a road, then enters a cutting (crossed above by a bridge) where there are two kinds of limestone, best seen at the far end of the cutting. The first is massive and forms tough bands of limestone. The other kind of limestone is 'rubbly', like lumpy porridge, on account of included clay material, concentrated into irregular bands, shown in Fig. 33. At Middleton Top, there is the old engine house (and tall chimney) which worked trains up and down the Incline, and the Middleton Visitor Centre, which has a small shop. There is a viewpoint direction indicator here, adjacent to the buildings. Opposite to the Visitor Centre, on the north side of the High Peak Trail, there is an access point to the disused Redhill Quarry, now a picnic site. Note the bedding and jointing* in the limestone here. There is a band of rubbly limestone near the base of the main quarry area. Fossils include crinoids and brachiopods.

Continue along the High Peak Trail, passing a road crossing, and enter the cutting leading into the short Hopton Tunnel. The first rocks encountered in the cutting, on the right-hand side (north) consist of limestones with nodules of chert*, as seen in Fig. 34, mostly white, but some black. This chert weathers proud of the general surface because of its relative insolubility in rainwater. Both the rubbly and the massive kinds of limestone are present here. There is another cutting on the far side of the tunnel where the

SCALE

Figure 33: Rubbly limestone, Middleton Incline, Middleton.
Scale bar = 10cm.

limestones show a pronounced easterly dip*. The High Peak Trail then continues past a working quarry on the right to reach the Hopton Incline, at the top of which is a small sculpture (in oolitic* limestone) mounted on a sandstone plinth and including a section of rail from the Cromford and High Peak Railway. Further along the High Peak Trail, Harboro' Rocks come into view to the right.

At the works on a level with Harboro' Rocks, there is a footpath

Figure 34: Chert in limestone; cutting near Bonsall Tunnel, High Peak Trail. Scale bar = 10cm

crossing. Turn right here, following the sign for 'Grangemill and Harboro Rocks'. Follow the path up on to the lower slopes of Harboro' Rocks and note the curious, castellated, towers (see Fig. 35) composed of dolomitised* limestone, rather brown in colour, and full of holes and cavities. The alteration has involved the incorporation of magnesium into the limestone causing the development of the mineral dolomite* (calcium magnesium carbonate). Dolomitised limestone is much less soluble than normal limestone. The calcite of some of the fossils apparently resisted alteration, but later was removed in solution, to leave their impressions (moulds*) in the rock. Such impressions are quite common. The question arises as to the origin of the magnesium that caused the dolomitisation. One possibility is that it was derived from overlying Permian strata, which have now been removed by erosion.

Walk to the right (east) under the line of crags to enjoy the scenery of these splendid rocks, then make for the summit triangulation point. There are good views from here, including that of Carsington Water to the south. From the triangulation point walk eastwards, taking care to avoid hidden hollows in the ground, to meet a track which leads north-eastwards, through a stile, to New Harboro' Farm.

Figure 35: Harboro' Rocks, Middleton. Dolomotised limestone.

Keep to the left of the farm and continue to the unmetalled road below. Here turn right, noting the dolomitised limestone in the walls. Continue, through gates, to the high point of the road then start a descent to reach two metal gates across the road. Note that changes have been made to the ground here and the 1:25 000 map needs revision. After the second gate, turn left along a track which is flanked on its right by a large dump of quarry waste. Dolomitised limestone is still an important constituent of the walls. Follow the path, through stiles, to reach a final steep descent to a road and farm on the valley floor.

Cross the road, pass the public footpath sign, and continue through the buildings and under the bridge (for a former mineral line to the quarry) to reach two stiles, the second being a wooden stile. The route beyond is not at first clear, but climb up to the hawthorn bush above, then head east-south-east towards a footpath sign post, then a double pole power line support. Moor Farm appears and should be approached. A road will be seen to the left of the first buildings. Take this roadway, pass through two gates then in a few metres, at a footpath sign on the right-hand side of the road, turn right and walk eastwards to meet a wire fence. The route follows this fence and passes old lead workings, including capped shafts. Footpath signs indicate the way forward, north-north-east, although the path is often quite indistinct. Eventually Middleton is reached via a straight length of roadway between walls. There is a surprise view of the town and its surroundings at the end of this road and a seat is provided for those wishing to stay awhile.

To the east is the prominent feature of Black Rock, formed of sandstone of Upper Carboniferous age, and a point soon to be visited on this walk. All the country to be seen beyond Black Rock is composed of the Upper Carboniferous, with the exception of an area around Crich – the monument of which can be seen in the same direction as, but beyond, Black Rock. At Crich, the Carboniferous limestone has been brought to the surface by an upfold (anticline) to provide a window through the cover of the surrounding Upper Carboniferous rocks. Such a 'window' is known as an inlier*. From the seat a path heads towards the north-west, contouring the hillside. Follow this path for about 60m, then turn right down a steep path into Middleton. Once into the houses a road junction will be met. Turn left here, down a steep road that leads to the main road through the village. Cross this road into Chapel Lane and in a few metres turn right, past the stonemason's yard, then the chapel, and out into the fields again. Middleton Hall appears on the left. Continue along this lane with its stiles, in an easterly direction, heading in the direction of the television mast on the high ground ahead (which is adjacent to Black Rock). The route crosses an area much disturbed by old lead workings (during the summer months, look for the Vernal Sandwort, or Leadwort, *Minuartia verna*, Fig. 9). Black Rock soon comes into view. Head in its direction. Cross the B5036 road to reach, first, the Steeple Arch Cemetery, and then the Black Rock Visitor Centre (information, toilets), just below the High Peak Trail.

At the Trail turn left (eastwards) and continue a few metres to the turn off for Black Rock. There is an information board here, with map. Take the right-hand of the two paths leading up to Black Rock and walk up to the exposure. This sandstone is the Ashover Grit (see Fig. 3) of Upper Carboniferous age and forms the cover to the limestones below. Note the stratification*. The hollows seen on weathered surfaces are carbonate concretions* where calcareous cement has been attacked by acid rain leading to the localised breakdown of the sandstone. The rest of the sandstone has a silica cement.

Below the main face at Black Rock there are tips of mine waste with pieces of limestone, lumps of black clayrock*, black siltstone* and mineral specimens such as calcite*. Some of the calcite specimens are of special interest because they show good mineral cleavage* features. It is clear that mine shafts were sunk through the Upper Carboniferous to reach mineral veins in the limestone. Walk up to the top of Black Rock for the views. Dene Quarry, in the limestone, lies below to the north-west, Cromford to the north, with Riber Castle beyond. The geological features here include well developed jointing*, the vertical breaks in the sandstone. Return to the High Peak Trail and walk towards the west, passing the start of the tourist Steeple Grange Railway, and back to the Middleton Stone Centre.

Walk 7: Dovedale

Limestone Scenery

Start of Walk: Car park at south end of Dovedale (SK 146 509).

Maps:
  Topographical: : 1:25 000 OS Explorer Map : OL1, The Peak District,
  White Peak Area.
  Geological: British Geological Survey 1:50 000 Sheet 124, Ashbourne
  (Solid and Drift Edition)

Distance: 7¼ miles (11.5km)

Refreshments: Snacks, toilets at the car park

From the car park take the path (which starts between the toilets and the shop) to head northwards between the road and the River Dove. The path converges with the road near a footbridge over the river. Cross the footbridge, ignore the left turn leading to a path along the river bank, and continue eastwards to walk along the southern flank of Thorpe Cloud, following the line of a limestone* wall. At a path junction (by a stile in the wall) turn left to make for the rather exciting summit ridge. This is an excellent vantage point to see Dovedale below. Examine the rock exposures in the summit rocks. Fossils of various kinds are to be seen. For instance, at the eastern end of the ridge the limestone exhibits stromatolites*, identified by the presence of concentric banding, shown in Fig. 37. Smoothed surfaces of the limestone are the best for finding stromatolites. These calcareous structures were constructed by cyanobacteria* (once referred to as Blue-green Algae), organisms closely related to bacteria but which utilised sunlight by means of photosynthesis. Stromatolites are amongst the most ancient forms of life known and date back some 3,000 million years (about three-quarters of the way back to the time of the origin of planet Earth). Stromatolites are being formed today, but are rarely preserved because of the activity of animals that ingest sediment for its food content. These sediment-feeders did not exist in earlier geological times.

On the north side of the western end of the summit ridge search for fossil shells, such as those in Fig. 38. These occur in small clusters in the limestone. They consist mainly of small species of brachiopods*, but a great variety of other groups is represented here, including snails (gastropods*), trilobites*, and bivalves*. The assemblage is unique and associates with carbonate mound or knoll reef*

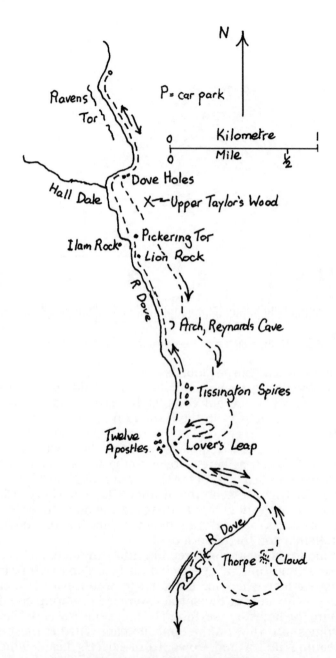

Figure 36: Sketch map of Dovedale

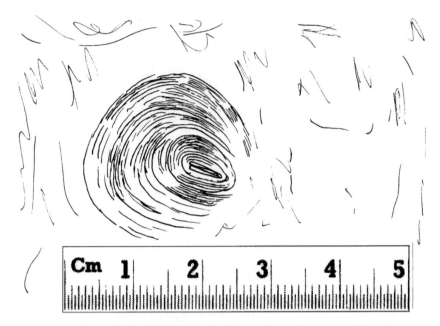

Figure 37: Stromatolites at the summit of Thorpe Cloud, Dovedale

limestone, of which Thorpe Cloud is made. These rocks can usually be recognised by the presence of poor, indistinct bedding. The origins of knoll reef limestone are not completely understood, but probably involved bacterial activity in the formation and cementation of the limestone. The knoll reef fossil assemblage is quite distinct from the large brachiopod-coral assemblage found in the 'shelf' limestones. The knoll reef limestone here belongs to the Milldale Limestone and so is close to the oldest beds of the Carboniferous Limestone exposed in the Peak District. Descend the northern flank of Thorpe Cloud to the River Dove, at the point where there are stepping stones (polished by numerous boots to reveal crinoid remains and brachiopods) across the river. Remain on the eastern bank.

Continue in an upstream direction into Dovedale, a spectacular example of a limestone valley which owes its origin to a time (during the Pleistocene*) when all subsurface water was frozen and occasional meltwaters at the surface were able to bring about deep erosion into the limestone surface. The limestone tower of 'Dovedale Castle' comes into view on the opposite bank. Further on there are steps (leading up to and down from Lover's Leap) which are

Figure 38: Brachiopods at the summit of Thorpe Cloud, Dovedale

constructed from limestone blocks rich in crinoid* remains and productoid brachiopods*. From Lover's Leap there is a good view of the limestone pinnacles of the Twelve Apostles across the river at certain times of the year. Beyond Lover's Leap look for trees with curved trunks, indicating growth on unstable ground. Continue past a wooden gate, a cave, then the high tors of Tissington Spires (mostly composed of knoll reef limestone) which are seen on the right. Note that the shape of the towers is controlled by the presence of joints* in the limestone. The pumphouse here (worked by water action) once pumped water up to the farmland above, another indication of the problem of water supply in limestone areas at some times of the year. Further along the route the large natural arch in front of Reynard's Cave appears on the right, before reaching the Lion Rock (in knoll reef limestone) which is so aptly named when approached from the south – see Fig. 39. Lush vegetation may hide this spectacular feature from the path in the spring and summer but a short ascent will be rewarded with a good view. Continue along the path the short distance to the towers of Pickering Tor (with a cave at its base), to the right of the path, and Ilam Rock, on the opposite bank of the River Dove. Both Ilam Rock and Pickering Tor are in knoll reef limestone, their form resulting from joints in the rock. There is a footbridge over the river here carrying the footpath to Stanshope.

From Ilam Rock the route continues to the caves known as Dove Holes. At this point it is worth taking a short detour to see a good example of knoll reef limestone and its lateral passage into well bedded Milldale Limestone (see Fig. 3). The detour continues along Dovedale in the upstream direction. Shortly, the cliff of Ravens Tor appears in the opposite bank of the River Dove. This cliff reveals the contact between knoll reef and non-reef limestone – see Fig. 40. Shortly beyond Ravens Tor, in a right bend of the track, there is an excellent exposure

Figure 39: The Lion Rock, Dovedale

of bedded limestone, readily distinguished from the 'reef'. This bedded limestone is rather dark in hue because of included clay material. Deposition of such limestone probably occurred in deeper water, where mud could settle, rather than on turbulent reef or shelf regions where deposition of mud would be more unlikely. Accordingly such limestones are referred to as of 'basin' type, or to use a geological term, of 'basin facies', the latter word meaning the sum of the rock's characteristics. Return to Dove Holes.

From Dove Holes walk past the caves, then, immediately, take a path to the left leading up into Upper Taylor's Wood. Care is needed to locate this track. There is a steady climb through the wood but, as height is gained, the vegetation thins to provide spectacular views

Figure 40: Ravens Tor, Dovedale. The passage from 'reef' to bedded limestone can be seen here.

into Dovedale below. Walk southwards across spurs and hollows, keeping to the high ground and close to the boundary wall above. The path is good in places, elsewhere becomes indistinct. Keep walking in the direction of Thorpe Cloud, seen in the distance. Most of the outcrops seen are of knoll reef limestone. Eventually the lower part of Dovedale comes into view, with Thorpe Cloud beyond. At this point follow the crest of the spur which runs down towards Lover's Leap, for views of Dovedale in general and the Twelve Apostles in particular. Then descend into the hollow on the north side of the spur to return along a footpath to the River Dove below, at Lover's Leap. There are exposures of bedded limestone ('basin facies') near the bottom of the track. Once at Lover's Leap walk back towards the stepping stones. Here remain on the same (left) bank of the river and continue below the slopes of Thorpe Cloud. The knoll reef limestone is well exposed here.

Cross the footbridge below Thorpe Cloud and return to the car park.

Walk 8: The Roaches, Lud's Church

Geology and Scenery

Start of Walk: Car parking at the Roaches Gate (SK 004 621)

Maps:
> Topographical: 1:25 000 OS Explorer Map:OL1, The Peak District, White
> Peak Area.
> Geological: British Geological Survey 1:25 000 Sheet SK 06, The Roaches
> and Upper Dove Valley. 1:50 000 Sheet 111, Buxton (Solid and Drift
> Edition)

Distance: 8½ miles (13.5km)

Refreshments: Pub and café in Upper Hulme

From the car park walk through the nearby gate, then eastwards up along the main path, ignoring the track which heads towards Rockhall Cottage (Don Whillans' Memorial Hut) on the left, below the impressive sandstone crags (Roaches Grit, Fig. 3). Note the view of Hen Cloud, the conspicuous hill (a superb dip* and scarp* feature) to the south-east, illustrated in Fig. 42. Continue past a solitary gate post and alongside a wall to a stile and path junction. Turn left up the path to the Roaches and look around at the scenery. Away to the east is Ramshaw Rocks, composed of the same sandstone* as on the Roaches. The view ahead to the Roaches reveals that the strata here dip down to the right (east), so must turn up again to appear at Ramshaw Rocks. The structure is that of a down fold or syncline* (in this case, the Goyt Syncline, a major structure in this part of the Peak District – see Fig. 6a). Hen Cloud is also composed of the Roaches Grit, but the strata here dip north (indicated by the direction of the dip slope). This indicates that the Goyt Syncline is tilted down (plunges*) to the north (note, however, that the plunge direction reverses in the vicinity of Whaley Bridge, so that it is to the south in Lantern Pike, Walk 18). Between the Roaches and Ramshaw Rocks there is higher ground formed by sandstone and other rocks which must overlie the Roaches Grit.

Head up towards two conspicuous gate posts in a gap. Jointing* is well developed in the rocks hereabouts and the joint* faces allow inspection of bedding features. These include cross-stratification*. The cross-stratification in some loose blocks indicates that they have come to rest upside down! Beyond the gate posts there is a clear view of the dip and slope topography of the Roaches, controlled by the easterly dip

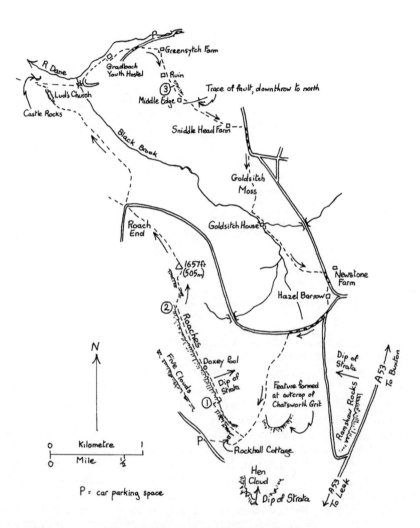

Figure 41: Sketch map of the Roaches area.

into the Goyt Syncline. Continue northwards below the crest line of the Roaches. This area is much frequented by rock climbers.

At one point (locality 1, Fig. 41) the path takes a sharp right turn and leads up to the top of the ridge. Just before reaching the crest, the path crosses the line of fault with the polished and scratched surfaces of the fault plain on the

Figure 42: Hen Cloud. Note the gradual dip slope down to the left and the steep scarp slope down to the right.

left. Such features are collectively known as slickensides*. It will be clear that fault movement here was horizontal and not vertical. Once on the summit ridge head northwards to pass Doxey Pool. Examine fresh specimens of the sandstone with a hand lens, to see (glassy) quartz* and (pink) feldspar* grains. The feldspars decay in contact with acidic water (notably peat water) to form kaolin clay, first becoming cloudy white before breaking down completely into clay. This clay is readily removed from the rock, which then appears porous, or may break down completely to release the quartz sand grains, so abundant in the path. Below to the west the features produced by the underlying Five Clouds Sandstone can be seen. Continue along the escarpment to a point directly above the northern limit of the wood below (locality 2, Fig. 41). Between this point and the summit of the Roaches, there are good examples of cross-stratification. In addition there are numerous holes and cavities in the sandstone (see Figs. 20, 27). These holes are explained by reference to the nature of the cement in the sandstone. Most of the sandstone is cemented by silica*, but there are patches which have a calcareous cement (calcium carbonate). Such patches are known as carbonate concretions*. These concretions are attacked by acid waters, when the cement is taken into solution, and the sand grains are released. The result of such weathering is the development of the holes and cavities, generally spherical or ovoid in shape and ranging in size from that of marbles to elephants.

Continue from the summit down to Roach End, passing superb wind-etched masses of sandstone. Sandstone flags have been laid here in the interest of footpath conservation. At Roach End cross the road and wall, turn right and take the path leading northwards downhill and into a wood. Turn left to follow a path close to upper boundary of the wood. Signs eventually indicate the route to the chasm of Lud's Church. Legend holds that the Lollards, a group of 14th century heretics, worshipped here. One of the leaders of the group was Walter de Lud-Auk. On reaching the chasm, keep left, follow the yellow way markers and descend the stone steps. The chasm is entered from the south-east, where it is about 3 metres wide, but it splits into subsidiary chasms towards the north-west. Lud's Church is a failed landslip. The rocks on the north-east side have moved downslope from those on the south-west side, the break occurring on joints in the sandstone. Walk through Lud's Church, then continue on a footpath which heads towards the north-west to meet another track and signpost, at a group of rocks known as Castle Rocks. Fissures here suggest that these rocks, too, were affected by landslip movement.

Follow the sign to 'Gradbach', descending through Forest Wood towards the east. Keep following 'Gradbach' signs to reach Black Brook, a tributary of the nearby River Dane. Descend to a footbridge, cross the brook, follow the path uphill, and pass through a stile (with the word 'FOOTPATH' engraved in stone) to a track. Here, turn left and follow the track down to the Dane valley, past a Scout camp site and on to Gradbach Youth Hostel (the site of the former Gradbach Mill). Beyond the hostel the track emerges through a rather splendid gateway (the entrance to the former mill) on to a road. Follow this road eastward for a few metres, then turn right at the sign for 'Greensytch Farm'. On the way to the farm examine the scenery on the far side of the Dane valley. The features (such as dip slopes*) formed by sandstones indicate that in this vicinity the dip of the strata is to the east, upstream. But in the distance this dip reverses and it is possible to identify the point at which this happens. This point is on the axis* of the Goyt Syncline.

Just before Greensytch Farm turn right, cross the footbridge into the field behind the farm, then walk uphill to a stile. Continue south-south-east and keep to the left of the ruined buildings that appear ahead. The same direction should be followed uphill along a poorly marked path which runs alongside a low ridge (scarp slope* of a sandstone, the Rough Rock (see Fig. 3), which here dips towards the east). The path then becomes enclosed by stone walls. Sandstone exposed here in small quarry workings (locality 3, Fig. 41) shows good examples of cross-stratification and, particularly, carbonate concretions. In the latter it is possible to follow the bedding from the host sandstone into the concretions, shown in Fig. 43. The ruin ahead is Middle Edge. The scarp feature here is broken by a notch, indicating the position of a small fault. Note that the level of the ground ahead, on the far side of the notch, is somewhat higher, so is on the upthrow side of the fault. Cross the fault. Do not enter the access the land ahead but turn south-eastwards on the dip slope of the Rough Rock, but with virtually no path. Continue until Sniddle Head Farm comes into view. Just beyond the farm, cross a stile and turn left onto the track. Go down the road and turn right.

Walk along this road in a southerly direction to a major left turn. Here a footpath continues southwards and leads on to Goldsitch Moss, which lies on the axis of the Goyt Syncline with dip slopes rising to left and right, respectively, on the limbs of the fold. There are numerous coal workings here in the form of bell pits*, well seen in the vicinity of two upstanding gate posts, shown in Fig. 44. The debris

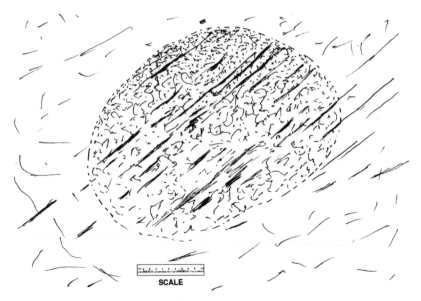

SCALE

Figure 43: Carbonate concretion in sandstone, with bedding passing from surrounding sandstone into the concretion. Scale bar = 10cm

associated with the bell pits is dominated by clayrocks*, but pieces of coal will also be seen. The seams worked lie above the level of the Yard Coal (Fig. 3). Head towards the buildings around Goldsitch House to the south, then pass by the buildings and turn right by the bridge to follow a path which runs alongside a stream, Black Brook (again). In the banks of the stream are exposures of black clayrocks, with evidence in places of coal workings. Boggy sections of the path provide opportunities to carry out the 'oil test'*! This area is noted for the richness of its birdlife. The path continues to a road below Newstone Farm. Note the dip slopes on this eastern limb of the Goyt Syncline, and the exposed sandstone crags to the east. Turn right on the road for a few metres, then at the point where power lines cross the road, turn right again for Hazel Barrow. This section of path cuts off a corner in the road which, when joined, should be followed to the right. In about 100 metres take the right fork, then after passing under more power lines watch for the cattle grid and broad track which leads off to the left for the Roaches. Avoid left turns along this track. Hen Cloud appears suddenly as the Roaches are approached. Walk to the car park.

Figure 44: Bell pits, Goldsitch Moss.

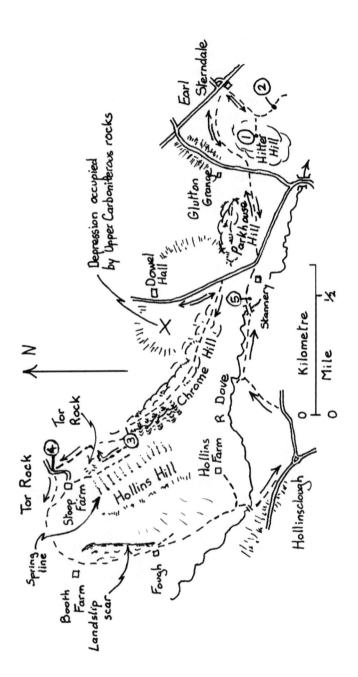

Figure 45: Sketch map of the Earl Sterndale - Hollinsclough area.

Walk 9: Earl Sterndale – Parkhouse Hill – Chrome Hill

Limestone 'Reefs'

Start of Walk: Parking in Earl Sterndale (SK 091 670)

Maps:
  Topographical: :25 000 OS Explorer: OL24, The Peak District, White Peak Area.
  Geological: British Geological Survey 1:25 000 Sheet SK 06, The Roaches and Upper Dove Valley 1:50 000 Sheet 111, Buxton (Solid and Drift Edition)

Distance: 6 miles (9.5km)

Refreshments: Pub in Earl Sterndale

Locate the 'Quiet Woman' (without a head!) on the lower (south) side of the village, then walk round the right (west) side of the building to take the path which climbs south-westwards towards Hitter Hill. Cross the stile at the top of the climb then leave the path to walk to the summit (locality 1, Fig. 45) of Hitter Hill, following a line of old lead workings. The view from the summit is most impressive, taking in Parkhouse Hill immediately to the west, then Chrome Hill beyond. The River Dove to the left marks the border between Staffordshire (far side) and Derbyshire.

Hitter, Parkhouse and Chrome Hills are formed largely of 'apron reef'* marking the limit of an early Carboniferous shelf sea which extended to the east (right) from here. Outcrops of limestone* in this direction reveal more or less flat stratification, indicating that little disturbance (apart from uplift!) has occurred since deposition. To the west, the shelf sea gave way to a deep basin in which mud as well as limestone accumulated. This basin has been buried beneath rocks of late Carboniferous age, comprising sandstones* and clayrocks* which form the hills seen on the far side (west) of the Dove. Erosion of the 'shelf edge' limestones in mid-Carboniferous times allowed the deposition of Upper Carboniferous clayrocks into erosional hollows in the limestone. Today these clayrocks are being eroded more rapidly than the limestones, resulting in such striking features as Glutton Dale (directly in front) and Dowel Dale (between Parkhouse and Chrome Hills). To see examples of stromatolites* in the apron-reef, rejoin the path and continue in the direction of the Dove valley. Immediately beyond the first stile (locality 2, Fig. 45) search the stones in the top of the wall, on the left, for stromatolites (for another example, see Fig. 37). Return to the 'Quiet Woman'.

On reaching the buildings of the 'Quiet Woman' turn left (west) to follow the path (signed for Hollins Clough) into Glutton Dale. Here cross the road, and continue the walk along the southern flank of Parkhouse Hill. The path soon joins a road coming in from the left. Within a few metres of this junction the road forks. Take the right fork to enter the gap between Parkhouse and Chrome Hills. This gap broadens out to form Dowel Dale, a hollow occupied by Upper Carboniferous clayrocks, surrounded by limestone. Cross the cattle-grid and walk a short distance along the road into Dowel Dale to get good views of both Parkhouse and Chrome Hills. Bedding in the limestone of Parkhouse Hill is seen to be poorly developed, but with high dips* of around 35°. These high angles of dip are interpreted as being original depositional dips, from the evidence of partial, geopetal*, infills (spirit levels, see Fig. 7) within the rock. These limestones form part of the apron reef*, along the edge of a shallow 'shelf' sea which lay to the east. Note the terracettes* (for another example, see Fig. 62) on Parkhouse Hill. Return to the cattle-grid.

A concessionary footpath (signed for 'High Edge via Chrome Hill') starts from the cattle-grid to follow the ridge up Chrome Hill. The route provides one of the most exciting walks in Derbyshire. At various places along the ridge there are good exposures of the apron-reef limestone. The ascent is steep in places, exposed, but not difficult. At one point there is a stile accompanied by a 'dog gate' of some interest. Nevertheless it should not be attempted in strong winds or in mist. Views of Parkhouse Hill (with its steeply dipping limestones) and the Dove Valley are stunning – see Fig. 46. To the north and north-east, the 'shelf' limestones, with their near-horizontal strata can be seen, especially in Hillhead Quarry (where joints are also conspicuous). A geological section is shown in Fig. 6b. From the summit of Chrome Hill there is a splendid view in all directions which includes Kinder Scout and Mam Tor to the north. To the west, nearby, is Hollins Hill, an escarpment composed of the Longnor Sandstone (see Fig. 3). This sandstone, like most sandstones, is permeable*, in that water can flow through it via joints and pore spaces. Here the Longnor Sandstone rests on clayrocks and siltstones* which are impermeable* and a spring line* is developed along the contact where water is forced to emerge at the surface, Fig. 47. The impermeable beds act like a damp-proof course. Note that the summits of hills around approach the same general level, a so-called

Figure 46: View of Parkhouse Hill from Chrome Hill.

Figure 47: View of Hollins Hill from Chrome Hill. Note the spring line.

'concordance of summit levels', suggesting that the present scenery results from erosion into what was once an uplifted plateau.

Descend the northern ridge of Chrome Hill, passing many crags and, at one place, a natural arch. As the descent continues note that the walls are now composed of a mixture of limestone and sandstone blocks, an indication that the Upper Carboniferous rocks are not far away. On leaving the Chrome Hill ridge by a steep section of the path (locality 3, Fig. 45) there are excellent exposures of the (depositional) dips of the apron reef. Below this steep section of the path a signpost indicates the way, to the north-west. At the foot of Hollins Hill outcrops of limestone can be seen, so the junction of the Lower and Upper Carboniferous must occur in the hillside above. The path continues past more outcrops of limestone which extend to the crags of Tor Rock. Here follow the path which climbs uphill then turns left (northwards) to pass to the east of Tor Rock. Outcrops of sandstone occur close to the path. These outcrops are shown on the Geological Survey map as part of a block down-faulted against the limestone. The path continues with a wall (a mix of limestone and sandstone blocks) to the right and shortly reaches a road where there is a signpost (Locality 4, Fig. 45). Follow the direction of 'Booth Farm'. The path is indistinct, but head south-westwards, walking to the right of a copse of trees, passing above Stoop Farm, then follow the footpath signposts until a stile allows access on to a farm road leading to Booth Farm.

At Booth Farm ignore the entrance road into the farm but continue in a southerly direction crossing a cattle grid and follow the bridleway. The walls now are constructed entirely of sandstone, so the boundary between Upper and Lower Carboniferous has been crossed. There are roadside exposures of sandstones and siltstones with evidence of much disturbance by landslips. Further along the path a cliff will be seen on the left with exposures of sandstone (the Longnor Sandstone, see Fig. 3). This cliff is a landslip face. The sandstone dips towards the west here (ie., towards the observer) and rests on unstable clayrocks and siltstones, a situation which gives rise to collapse (a similar but more spectacular landslip is seen at Coombes Rocks, Walk 18, Fig. 73). As the walk continues, note the hummocky ground produced by landslips in the vicinity of the path.

Keep to the left of 'Fough' cottage then, at the fork in the path just beyond, keep to the right. Continue the walk past a metal gate (stile alongside) shortly beyond which a left bend brings into sight the Upper Dove valley and Parkhouse Hill. A few metres beyond the bend a notice indicates that the track ahead is on private land. It is necessary here to take the path that leads off to the right. Follow the yellow markers which lead to an unusual stile with a white gate, then a footbridge over the River Dove. Once across the bridge look at the banks of the stream to note outcrops of clayrocks, here stained orange and red by the oxidation of iron minerals such as pyrite*. From the bridge, turn left and follow the path uphill to join a road and turn left to the hamlet of Hollinsclough.

At the triangular green in Hollinsclough turn left (east), pass the chapel and school, then at a right bend in the road take the track leading off to the left. This track heads directly towards Chrome Hill, to reach the River Dove. Here the path splits. Turn right to walk alongside the river in a downstream direction. The track crosses the Dove (by both ford and footbridge) and just beyond the crossing point (locality 5, Fig. 45) is an exposure of (Upper Carboniferous) clayrocks, very dark on account of contained organic matter. In this area many fossil bands with remains of marine shells indicate that these rocks were formed as sediments on a sea floor. The path continues past Stannery Farm and rejoins the road which passes between Parkhouse and Chrome Hills. Retrace steps to Earl Sterndale.

Walk 10: Lyme Park – Cage Hill – Bowstones

Sandstones, Glacial features

Start of Walk: Car park, Lyme Hall (SJ 963 823)

Maps:
> Topographical: 1:25 000 OS Explorer Map: OL1, The Peak District, Dark Peak Area
> Geological: British Geological Survey 1:50 000 Sheet 98, Stockport (Solid Edition and Drift Edition) 1:50 000 Sheet 99, Chapel-en-le-Frith (Solid Edition and Drift Edition)

Distance: 3½ miles (5.5km)

Refreshments: Café open daily 11am – 4pm throughout the year. Phone 01663 762 023 to check times.

There is an Information Centre alongside the car park. At the south-west corner of the Centre is a sandstone* slab with parting lineation* – see Fig. 12b. Walk across the car park in the direction of the café and toilets. Within a triangular area of grass (locality 1, Fig. 48) there are blocks of sandstone, one of which has fossil plant material preserved as impressions (for another example see Fig. 25).

From the car park walk up towards Lyme Hall. Note that the wall alongside the path is built of sandstone very similar to that seen already. At the gates to the Hall note the sandstone setts* (blocks of stone formerly used in roadways). Walk away from the Hall, following the road which leads up to a small cutting only a few metres away. There is an exposure of sandstone (the Milnrow Sandstone, see Fig. 3) in this cutting. Note that the stratification* has a steep dip*, of about 65° towards the west. This dip is partly due to tilting of all the rocks in this area, partly due to oblique bedding (cross-stratification*) already in these rocks before tilting, illustrated in Fig. 49. Another feature here is that all the bedding has been steepened immediately below the soil level. This terminal curvature* results from the action of soil creep, in this case down to the left.

From the cutting walk up the slope in the direction of the Cage and Cage Hill. About 70-75 metres from the cutting (locality 2, Fig. 48) there is a large boulder, adjacent to a marker post (for orienteers) bearing the number 35. The boulder is not composed of sandstone, but of granite*. Such rocks were formed from molten material, which cooled to form the interlocking mineral grains seen here. The minerals quartz* (dark grey), and feldspar* (pink) can be seen, possibly flaky mica* (shiny, flaky), too. This granite is identical in composition and texture to the Eskdale Granite of the Lake District.

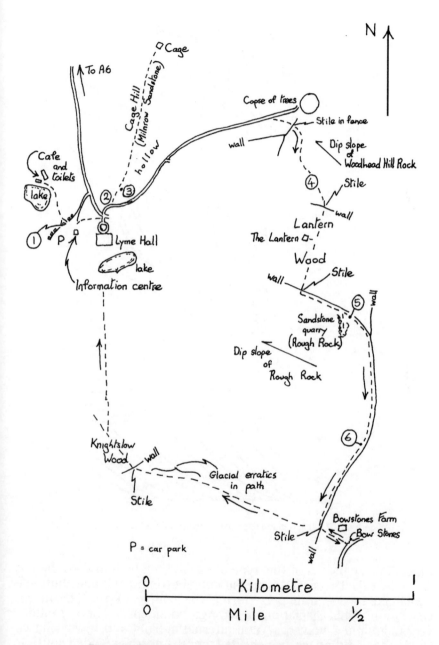

Figure 48: Sketch map of the Lyme Hall - Bowstones area.

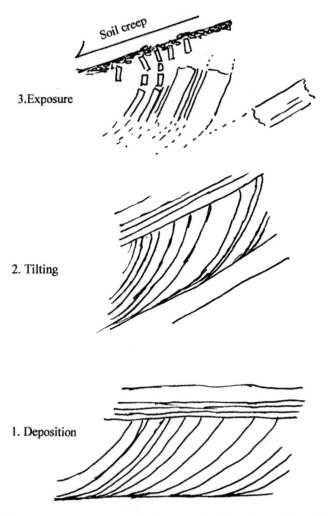

Figure 49: The origin of the tilted beds opposite the entrance to Lyme Hall.

Indeed, loose blocks of this type of granite can be found all the way from the Lake District to Lyme Park and beyond. Their distribution is explained by ice transport during the course of the Pleistocene Glaciation*. This Glaciation, or Ice Age, commenced about 2 million years ago and involved several alternating cold and warm phases. During the cold phases ice sheets from the north extended south to the Peak District and beyond. The last cold phase (Devensian) ended about 10,000 years ago. Between the cold phases the climate was as warm, or warmer, than it is today. The ice will probably come back at some stage in the future.

Continue along the crest of Cage Hill in the direction of the Cage, for about 150 metres, to a second boulder, on the left (west) side of the track (locality 3, Fig. 48). This boulder is composed of neither sandstone, nor granite. The rock type here is volcanic and was formed as an ash deposit which, now consolidated, is known as 'tuff'. Although the boulder is weathered it is possible to see angular fragments of volcanic material. The weathering has led to the development of a white or light-grey skin caused by the formation of the white clay mineral kaolinite* within feldspars in the rock. In this area many such boulders of volcanic rocks are to be found. Some of them are tuffs, as here, but others are composed of lava. The range of volcanic material found matches the range of volcanic rocks found in the central part of the Lake District. These rocks belong to the Borrowdale Volcanic Group. As with the Eskdale Granite, these Borrowdale volcanic boulders were transported here during the Ice Age. Blocks such as these boulders are described as erratics*, distinguished by being composed of rocks different from those of the district in which they are found.

Note that Cage Hill is a long ridge, formed by the outcrop of the Milnrow Sandstone – see Fig. 3. The sandstone dips* towards the west (in the direction of the Cheshire Plain). Rocks less resistant to erosion, such as clayrocks* and siltstones* (examples to be seen later) crop out on both sides of Cage Hill so the topography there is lower. In Lyme Park all the sandstone outcrops correspond to ridges (escarpments*) and all the clayrocks and siltstones to hollows and low ground.

From Cage Hill walk eastwards, across the hollow formed over softer rocks, to meet a roadway. Turn left, ignore a side road which turns off to the right (with a cattle grid) and continue towards a copse of trees directly ahead. Note the point at which a stone wall on the right terminates. Before reaching the copse turn right along a path which heads towards a stile with a high post, close to the wall termination. Cross the stile, then climb obliquely up the hill slope in front (locality 4, Fig. 48) in a south-easterly direction. Although sandstone chippings have been introduced here it is evident that at some stage the ground has been disturbed and much sandstone material brought to the surface from beneath the soil level. There is clearly sandstone beneath. The hill being climbed is part of a ridge, formed by the outcrop of the Woodhead Hill Rock, the next sandstone down in the sequence beneath the Milnrow Sandstone (see Fig. 3). The sandstone fragments are worth close study. In many cases they appear to be rough and full of small holes or pits. Here, feldspar grains have been broken down to form clay minerals (as was happening in the Borrowdale Volcanic erratic seen on Cage Hill) and removed leaving pores and cavities. The rock left is composed of mainly quartz grains and the natural rock cement (silica). The main agent of feldspar weathering is acid and in this case humic acids from the soil are probably responsible.

Cross a prominent stile ahead and enter Lantern Wood. The path beyond is composed of sandstone chippings. Accumulations of mica grains, transparent and shiny, can be seen on some of the chippings. Note the variation in colour of the chippings ranging from a lighter to a darker brown. This variation is produced by different stages of weathering. When fresh, these sandstones are practically white, but with weathering the small amount of iron in the rock is converted to a natural rust (iron oxides and hydroxides), thereby making the rock darker in colour.

Continue along the path through the wood to the Lantern, a small sandstone folly with a hexagonal tower, on the right. From the Lantern there is a good view of Lyme Hall. Inside the tower there are good examples of fossil ripple marks in the sandstone flags. In the patio area, outside the tower, note the two (largest) flags with parting lineation*. Return to the path in Lantern Wood and continue southwards to the stile over a sandstone wall. Turn left, uphill, towards the abandoned sandstone (Rough Rock, see Fig. 3) quarry entrance indicated by the marker post 55. Walk into the quarry and look for fresh specimens of coarse-grained sandstone ('grit'). Grains of feldspar (pink), quartz (grey) and mica (flaky) can be seen. They are now cemented together by quartz. Samples of weathered sandstone will also be seen, where the feldspar has been removed to produce the pitted appearance seen earlier. The sandstone is well exposed in the quarry and can be seen to slope down ('dip') to the right (west), so must underlie the slope of the hillside (such slopes being known, therefore, as dip slopes*). Within individual beds or strata, cross-stratification* can be seen. The direction of stream flow, as determined from a number of examples of cross-stratification in this quarry, was from a northerly direction. The Rough Rock was formed as a sheet of sand, deposited in the form of sand banks, etc., in the streams of a vast delta during the Carboniferous, about 320 million years ago.

Return to post 55 and continue uphill. About 20 metres from the quarry entrance (locality 5, Fig. 48), note the small block of sandstone in the path, with a fine impression of a fossil plant, probably *Lepidodendron* (see Fig. 4d). Such plant impressions are relatively common and represent plant material washed down into the delta by rivers. Continue uphill to reach a junction of walls, at which point there is a good view to the east. From here the plateau of Kinder Scout can be seen, formed by a flat-lying bed of thick sandstone known as the Kinderscout Grit (see Fig. 3). This sandstone, together with the Rough Rock, belongs to a succession of strata within the Carboniferous known as the Millstone Grit Series because they were once the source of stone used in the manufacture of millstones. To the left of Kinder Scout and above New Mills, Cown Edge can be seen as an escarpment* produced by the westerly dip of the Rough Rock. In the middle distance, and across the valley to the east, behind the hotel, is Black Rocks, also an escarpment of the Rough Rock, but where the dip direction is in the opposite direction to that of the dip in the quarry just visited. So the view to Black Rocks is across the axis of an upfold or anticline* (the Todd Brook Anticline, see Fig. 6a), where erosion has removed the top of the fold. There is a fault along the line of the axis of the fold here, but the evidence for the fault is not visible from the viewpoint.

Follow the high wall southwards to the Memorial to the children of Alan Monkhouse (locality 6, Fig. 48). There is a view indicator here. In the Cheshire Plain to the west the Carboniferous rocks are hidden beneath the New Red Sandstones of the Permo-Triassic*. To the north-west is Manchester, nearer is Lyme Hall. The low ridges near the Hall are escarpments of sandstone. The low ground between escarpments is formed from the more-easily eroded clayrocks and siltstones.

Approaching Bowstones Farm the view to the south reveals a number of ridges, each formed by underlying sandstones, the hollows in between by clayrocks, siltstones and thin coal seams. At Bowstones turn left (eastwards) to reach the road and the two Bow Stones, the shafts of Saxon crosses. There is an explanatory notice about the stones here. The view to the south-east takes in the Todd Brook Valley, flanked by escarpments which show that the sandstones here form a part of the anticline seen earlier. Shutlingslow, the 'Matterhorn' of the Peak District, is capped by sandstone (Rough Rock). All around Shutlingslow the Rough Rock has been removed by erosion. Such a remnant is known as an outlier*. Away to the east the limestones of the White Peak can be seen, if the weather is fine.

From Bowstones Farm, head westwards down the path leading to Knightslow Wood. Watch for the first appearance of glacial erratics, indicating the levels on this hillside to which the ice reached. Many erratics will be seen as the gate is approached at the bottom of the path. Pass through the gate and walk along the path, for about 200 metres. Here take the right fork to walk down the avenue to the Hall, passing marker 14. At the end of the avenue, by the Hall, turn left into the car park.

Walk 11: Lyme Park – West Parkgate

Glacial Spillway, Fossil Soils and Fossil Ripple marks

Start of Walk: Car park, Lyme Hall (SJ 963 823)

Maps:

Topographical: 1:25 000 OS Explorer Map: OL1, The Peak District, Dark Peak Area

Geological: British Geological Survey 1:50 000 Sheet 98, Stockport (Solid Edition and Drift Edition) 1:50 000 Sheet 99, Chapel-en-le-Frith (Solid Edition and Drift Edition)

Distance: 3 miles (5km)

Refreshments: Café open daily 11am – 4pm throughout the year. Phone 01663 762023 to check times.

If this walk is done instead of Walk 10, please see the description of the start of Walk 10 for information about the geology to be seen in the car park!

Follow the road leading southwards from the car park, noting the blocks of the local (Carboniferous*) sandstone* on the right-hand side of the road. The road bends to the right and climbs to a summit in a shallow cutting. On the right-hand side of the road (locality 1, Fig. 50) look for exposures (which vary in extent from time to time) of clay with pebbles and cobbles of rock. Appropriately, this material is known as Boulder Clay*. Many of the enclosed rocks are of a local type, like the sandstones seen along the road, but other rocks are quite unlike any rocks of this area. These strange rocks are known as erratics* and they include rock types identical in type with rocks found in the Lake District and in southern Scotland. These erratics were brought here by ice during the last of the Pleistocene Glaciations (Ice Age)*, when ice sheets spread from the north and crossed this area on several occasions during the last 2 million years. Walk to the road junction, take the left fork and continue to a clump of six trees (locality 2, Fig. 50). The road beyond continues into a dry valley – a valley with no stream. This valley is interpreted as a glacial meltwater spillway, i.e., it was formed by powerful erosion when large quantities of water were produced by melting ice. Such water may have flowed beneath the ice, or along ice margins, forming lakes on the way. The evidence on the ground in this case suggests ice-margin flow. To the right is the Knott, formerly an island in the spillway.

From the trees leave the road and cross the rough ground in an easterly direction for a few metres to meet a track leading towards the south-east and a wall junction. Cross the stile in the wall junction. Immediately beyond the stile the path forks. Take the right-hand fork to climb obliquely past a post marked PT (Pemberley Trail) to the crest of the hill. Walk along the crestline (locality 3, Fig. 50) to view the glacial spillway below. Then continue southwards along the path to Paddock Cottage (locality 4, Fig. 50), which has been on this site since at least the 17th century. Here, parting lineation* (see Fig. 12b) is seen in two of the sandstone flags, near the doorway. From the Cottage look eastwards to see outcrops of (dark) clayrocks* and siltstones* in the valley below. These clayrocks continue beneath the sandstone of the ridge upon which the Cottage stands. To the west there is a good view of the Cheshire Plain, where the Carboniferous rocks lie buried beneath thick deposits of the New Red Sandstone of Permo-Triassic* age. To the south the ridges are formed by outcrops of sandstones, the hollows by outcrops of less-resistant rocks like clayrocks and siltstones.

Follow the crest line of the hill to the south. Reach two oak trees (locality 5, Fig. 50) next to an impressive outcrop of sandstone where there are good examples of fossil ripple marks*. The chances of preservation of such structures as these are remote. Generally such structures are washed away soon after formation. To be preserved they need to be covered by a layer of mud and buried before destruction can take place. Subsequent uplift and exposure allows erosion of the (softer) clayrock cover to reveal the ripples beneath.

Continue along the path with a deep valley to the left. The path is joined, for a short distance, by a wire fence which comes in from the right. The walk involves a steady descent. Near the bottom (at the junction with the spillway channel) the path steepens as it crosses an outcrop of siltstone and enters the trees. Just above the partially exposed area of tree roots of a large oak tree (locality 6, Fig. 50) the rocks contain fossil roots and represent an ancient soil. Such a rock is known as a seatearth* (see Fig. 4a, b). This frequently occurs beneath coal seams in this district and elsewhere. In addition to the root structures which cut across the bedding of the rock there are fossilised plant stems (ie., formed above ground and not part of the root system) which lie along the bedding. The question arises as to how roots and stems can be fossilised in the same rock. The explanation is that the stems were buried in the sediment first. Then, new plants were established and their roots penetrated down to the level of the sediment containing stems. Therefore, the fossils seen here are not all of the same age!

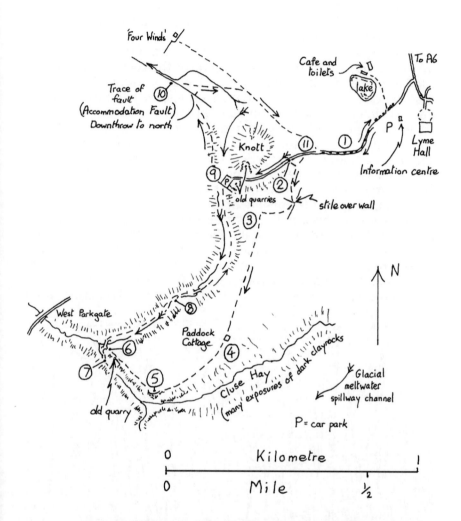

Figure 50: Sketch map of the Lyme Hall - West Parkgate area.

The ground below the oak tree is steep. Use the roots as a staircase to descend to a path below and turn left to see a small quarry, which reveals a section of the rocks just seen beneath the oak tree. Look for pieces of rock in this quarry to see more examples of seatearth. Pass through two stone posts and continue for a few metres to a point (locality 7, Fig. 50) where the stream is seen to flow over an extensive bedding plane of sandstone. This surface is made of superb fossil ripple marks. Their form is remarkably similar to that of modern ripples and shows that little distortion has occurred during the 300 million years that they have been in the rock. Walk a short distance upstream to inspect the stratification* of the rocks here. There are sandstones and siltstones, which all dip* towards the west. The association with fossil soils and plants suggests that these rocks were once sediments deposited on land, probably in lagoons or in river channels. The sands represent deposition under more turbulent conditions, the siltstones and clayrocks under more tranquil conditions. Note the flat vertical breaks, or joints*, in these rocks. Joints are associated with rocks near the surface and are developed as erosion removes the load of overburden, allowing the rocks to expand, mainly by the opening up of joints.

Retrace steps back to the oak tree and the spillway channel. Turn right (north) towards Lyme Hall. The slopes of the spillway channel are steep. Note that many of the trees on these slopes show a distinct curvature of the trunk near the base of the tree. This is due to soil creep* and the rotation of young trees as they grow. The curvature results from a correction to the tilt, shown in Fig. 51. Further up the

Figure 51: Trees with curved trunks as evidence of unstable ground.

spillway a track leads off to the right (locality 8, Fig. 50). Walk a metre or so up this path and, adjacent to a 'no cycling' notice, a surface with ripple marks will be seen, somewhat eroded by walkers and vehicles. Look carefully at these ripples. Small scale bedding (lamination*) within the ripples allows the direction of water flow to be determined, in this case from south-west to north-east. Return to the main path and continue to the gate and stile where the track meets a car park.

At the gate turn left (west) to follow the stone wall up the hillside to a small terrace (locality 9, Fig. 50) from which a good view can be had of the Knott and the spillways on either side (the far one with the road through it) shown in Fig. 52. Head northwards from this point (a compass is useful). Climb over the crest of the hill in front, then walk in the direction of the conspicuous white house ('Four Winds') beyond. A stream gully will be seen ahead. Walk to the deer fence and look down into the valley below and to the west. The stream banks are here composed of different kinds of rock – producing a marked contrast in colour, light grey on the far bank, nearly black on the near bank. The stream here flows along the line of a fault*, the Accommodation Fault. The rocks on the far bank have been dropped down relative to those of the near bank. At the top of the near bank

Figure 52: Glacial meltwater channel, Lyme Park.

exposures of the clayrocks reveal the presence of poorly preserved fossil mussel* shells. These shells are mostly represented by impressions (moulds*) left after the shell substance has been removed by weathering processes. The shells are oval in form and are about 2 cm in length. They can also be seen in cross section on joint faces of the rock, as well as on bedding planes. They were probably freshwater shells of creatures that lived in the lagoons and lakes of the time.

Walk eastwards to regain higher ground and follow the stream system towards its source. Join the main track which leads from 'Four Winds', alongside the stone wall north of the stream, towards Lyme Hall. In this track there are many rock types, including the local sandstones, but also glacial erratics, especially representatives of the Borrowdale Volcanic Group and the pink Eskdale Granite.

Continue to the junction of the roads at signpost 32 (locality 11, Fig. 50), where there are four blocks of sandstone. The first block encountered (ie., the most westerly) has a dished surface upon which are small raised lumps of sandstone. The dished surface is actually the under-surface ('sole surface') of a sandstone bed, which rested on an erosion surface cut on clayrocks or siltstones beneath. Scouring produced hollows in the clay or silt and, on deposition, sand filled the hollows to produce the lumps seen.

Return to the car park.

Walk 12: Lathkill Dale

Limestones, Fossils and Lead Mines

Start of Walk: Car park, both sides of road, B5055, near Monyash (SK 157 664)

Maps:
Topographical: 1:25 000 OS Explorer Map: OL24, The Peak District White Peak Area
Geological: British Geological Survey 1:25 000 Sheet SK16, Monyash. 1:50 000 Sheet 111, Buxton (Solid and Drift Edition)

Distance: 8 miles (14km)

Refreshments: in Over Haddon, toilets available at the car parking area

---

Take the track leading south-eastwards into the dry valley* forming the top of Lathkill Dale. Such dry valleys were formed during the Pleistocene Glaciation* or Ice Age, when all the ground water was frozen but when meltwater generated in large volumes by spring and summer melting caused much surface erosion. There are numerous outcrops of nearly horizontal limestone* beds on both sides of the dale. Fossils here, as well as elsewhere in the limestone, indicate deposition under the sea. The limestones are well stratified due to the presence of thin clay partings. Beyond the second gate (locality 1, Fig. 53) an exposure of limestone to the right (south side) of the path shows an interesting area of limestone 'pavement', with deep fissures (grikes*) separating blocks (clints*), all formed by solution of limestone along joint* systems. Such features are described collectively as 'karst'* scenery.

Just before the second gate take the footpath which leads up the left (northern) side of the Dale, following a wire fence. At the top of the hill is a good viewpoint from which to see along Lathkill Dale, almost canyon-like here, and Ricklow Quarry to the left (east), the next destination. Drop down into Ricklow Dale at a point north-west of Ricklow Quarry. On reaching Ricklow Dale note that the limestones on the far side of the dale show inclined bedding, as in Fig. 54. These limestones were accumulated over mounds or knoll reefs* on the sea floor and the bedding slopes down away from the top of each mound. The origin of the mounds is not fully understood, but it is probable that bacterial action may have caused cementation of the lime sediment to form seafloor material locally more resistant to being reworked by sea-floor

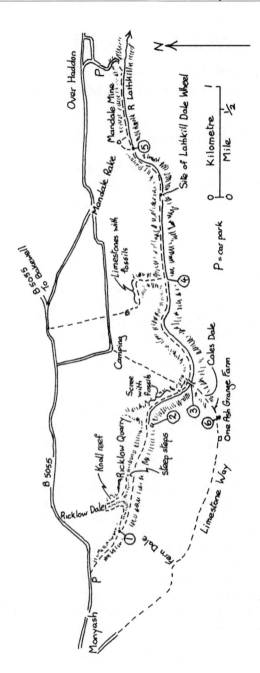

Figure 53: Sketch map of Lathkill Dale.

Figure 54: Knoll reef structures, Ricklow Dale.

currents than in the surrounding area. Accumulation of limestone on top of the mounds results in inclined bedding, sloping away from the top of each dome.

Descend into Ricklow Dale, turn right and follow the path alongside Ricklow Quarry until Lathkill Dale comes into view. At this point turn left a few metres into the quarry workings, along a former quarry roadway. Limestone outcrops to the right reveal a spectacular display of crinoidal* limestone, shown in Fig. 55. Many of the crinoids have been silicified* so are more resistant to weathering than the surrounding limestone. In some of the crinoids the central cavity has been partially infilled with limestone sediment, so that the top of the infill acts as a spirit level. Such partial infills are known as geopetal infills* (see also Fig. 7b). It will be seen that the limestone beds in the quarry were deposited as horizontal layers, but in the beds associated with the knoll reefs, as seen in Ricklow Dale, the 'spirit levels' show that the limestones there were deposited on slopes of up to about 30°. Adjacent to the crinoid locality there are many loose blocks of crinoidal limestone, also some blocks with parallel drill holes (see Fig. 56) which facilitated the breakage of the rock along straight lines to produce building blocks. Breakage was achieved with the use of a wedges ('plugs') between sleeves ('feathers'), the so-called 'plug and

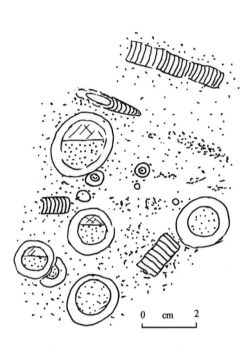

Figure 55: Crinoids with partial sediment infills, Ricklow Quarry.

feather' technique. There is a 'Keep-Out, Danger' notice further along this quarry roadway. Take note!

Continue along the path towards Lathkill Dale. At first the path contours along the top of the dale, then descends a steep set of steps, providing stunning views of Lathkill Dale to the left – see Fig. 57. Join the path at the bottom to walk down Lathkill Dale and immediately cross a stone stile, in which there are many fossils. Shortly the path crosses a rock fall derived from the southern side of the dale. Note that the largest blocks in the fall travelled furthest, a common feature of rock falls. The stratification* of the limestones hereabouts is well developed, and practically horizontal. The vertical flat faces on the limestone have been developed along the joints* in the limestone and these joints have controlled the development of the dale. Screes will be seen in many places and it is clear that their presence has produced the U-shaped profile of the valley. A small cave is met on the right-hand side of the dale (locality 2, Fig. 53) and water may or may not be flowing here, depending on the season.

A short distance beyond the cave a large tributary valley enters from the left (north). On the south side of the main dale note the terracettes*, small horizontal ledges on the grassy slopes, caused by soil creep (for another example see Fig. 62). Beyond the tributary the main valley takes a gentle right turn. In and beyond the bend the limestone strata in the slopes to the left (north-east) show that some beds are more resistant to weathering than others. These tougher beds contain less clay 'impurity' than the less resistant beds. The screes close to the path should be examined closely. Most of the scree is composed of limestone fragments, essentially angular in form. But

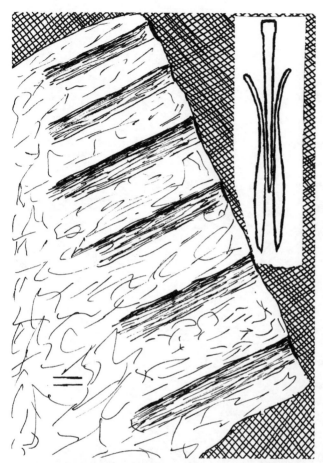

Figure 56: Holes drilled to break rock along straight fractures with use of 'plugs and feathers'. A plug and two feathers are illustrated separately.

there is also chert*, where silica* has replaced original limestone. The chert is much harder than the limestone and cannot be scratched by a knife blade. Look for specimens of both limestone and chert containing fossils, including crinoids*, corals*, and brachiopods*. In dry weather, the River Lathkill emerges at the surface here. A bridge over the river is reached at locality 3, Fig. 53. Ignore the bridge and continue downstream to enter a wooded area. The steps in one of the stiles along the path contain interesting brachiopods. The path passes a notice with information about the Lathkill Dale National Nature Reserve, then two weirs, the second of which was a dam to supply water for the former Carter's Mill, the only remains of which are two millstones on your left (locality 4, Fig. 53).

At this point it is possible to shorten the walk by heading up the tributary valley to the north. In that case, skip the next two paragraphs!

Figure 57: Lathkill Dale

The main walk continues down Lathkill Dale. The path enters a wood and follows a straight stretch of the River Lathkill. Before a left bend in the river, a large hollow on the river side of the track marks the site of a wheelpit, used for a waterwheel (Lathkilldale Wheel, 16m or 52 feet diameter) which provided power for mine drainage. Note the curved tree trunks* around here (see Fig. 51), caused by soil creep*. In this vicinity there is also a disused mine shaft, covered by a metal grid, which allows a view down into the shaft. About 250 metres after the bend in the river (locality 5, Fig. 53) the remains of the pillars which supported an aqueduct over the River Lathkill will be seen. This aqueduct carried water from a point upstream on the river to drive a waterwheel at the mine. Leave the main path to follow the rough track up the hill along the line of the former aqueduct and leat to the site of the mine. A metal grid now seals a small entrance to the workings, on the site of the original main mine entrance. Mandale Mine worked the Mandale Rake ('rake' is a local name for a vertical or near-vertical vein of ore) for lead ore (galena*, lead sulphide, PbS). There is an explanatory diagram (by English Nature) on site. Note the location of the former wheel pit where a 10.5m or 35 feet diameter water wheel operated to raise water from the workings. The water wheel was eventually replaced by a steam beam engine and there are impressive remains of the engine house. Water raised by the pumps was delivered to the Mandale Sough, a drainage tunnel, driven mainly between 1797 and 1851. This sough* followed the rake north-westwards for over a mile to collect water from other working areas. The 'tail' or 'outfall', of the sough, where the water empties into the River Lathkill, can be seen below. Mandale Mine was already working in the 13th century and is one of the oldest mines in the area. It closed in 1851.

From Mandale Mine it is about half a mile to Over Haddon where refreshments are available. On the way, look out for two trial workings on the left of the footpath. Return to the remains of Carter's Mill, at locality 4, Fig. 53.

From the Carter's Mill site leave Lathkill Dale to follow the path up into an unnamed tributary dale to the north. Close to the start of this path, on the left, is an old quarry, rather overgrown, with beds of limestone and black chert. Continue up the path, looking for fossils in loose blocks of limestone. Large productoid* brachiopods can be seen here in abundance. Once round a tight left bend near the top of the valley note the outcrops of limestone immediately to the right of the path. This limestone contains an abundance of brachiopod valves, mostly productoids. Each shell originally had a thicker valve below and a thinner valve above, both concave upwards, so resembling the appearance of two saucers, one sitting inside the other. It is possible to distinguish between the two valves at this outcrop. Many of these fossils have been silicified so that they stand proud of the limestone matrix which weathers more readily. Elsewhere it is the matrix rather than the fossils which have been silicified, so here the fossils have been selectively removed by solution. Stacking* is to be seen here, see Fig. 58, where a number of brachiopod valves have been trapped together like a pile of saucers, a phenomenon indicative of

0   cm   2

Figure 58: 'Stacking' with brachiopod valves.

accumulation under turbulent (storm) conditions. Continue up the path, past the farm buildings, to the minor road. Turn left for about 250 metres, then left again into the campground of Haddon Grove Farms. The route through the campground is not obvious at first, but head south-westwards to reach a stunning viewpoint over Lathkill Dale, directly above the footbridge at locality 3, Fig. 53. Descend the steep, but interesting, track down to the footbridge.

Cross the footbridge at locality 3, Fig. 53, and walk up Cales Dale, keeping to the west side of the valley to meet the 'Limestone Way'. Continue westwards towards One Ash Grange Farm. Before reaching the farm and to the left of the path (locality 6, Fig. 53), there is a mine entrance with a well exposed mineral vein in its roof. Calcite* crystals can be seen showing good mineral cleavage*. At One Ash Grange Farm note the limestone wall construction, slate roofs and sandstone quoins and lintels. From the farm the Limestone Way continues to the west-north-west, involving at least one stile where there are superb crinoid remains in the limestone blocks. In the vicinity of Fern Dale the path crosses an unnamed mineral vein (rake*) the line of which is picked out by old workings and dumps. Just beyond Fern Dale two stiles reveal superb crinoids, in one case nicely polished by the action of hikers' boots. The walk now continues as a roadway between stone walls. As Monyash comes into view, look for a stile on the right-hand side (no signpost). This stile gives access to a path leading directly into the village, from which it is only a short distance back to the parking area.

Walk 13: Goyt's Moss – Shining Tor

Sandstone Scenery and Coal

Start of Walk: Car park at Goyt's Moss: (SK 018 716)

Maps:

Topographical 1:25 000 OS Explorer Map: OL24, The Peak District White Peak Area

Geological: British Geological Survey 1:25 000 Sheet SK 07, Buxton. 1:50 000 Sheet 111, Buxton (Solid and Drift Edition)

Distance: 7¼ miles (11.5km)

Refreshments: at the 'Cat and Fiddle' Inn, toilets available at the car parking area

---

At the car park there is a notice which includes geological and other information. From the car park walk to the nearby road junction, adjacent to the bend in the River Goyt, and on in the direction that you came from. Continue past the next road junction, but then walk over to the river bank (locality 1, Fig. 59) where sandstone* will be seen in the stream bed. This sandstone is known as the Woodhead Hill Rock (and, elsewhere, as the Crawshaw Sandstone) – see Fig. 3. Note that the sandstone dips* slightly to the east, being on the western limits of the Goyt Syncline* and in the same direction as the flow of the River Goyt. Walk back downstream along the river bank until a fence prevents further access. It will be seen from here that the sandstone is overlain by a succession dominated by clayrocks*, well exposed in a cliff above the stream. Formerly it was possible to examine this succession in detail. A coal seam, the Yard Coal, was seen to lie between the sandstone and the clayrocks. This seam has been heavily worked in this area, in bell pit* workings and by pillar and stall* mining, the main period of working being between the end of the 18th century and the end of the 19th century. The outcrops of coal in the banks of the River Goyt here are abandoned coal pillars. An outcrop of this seam may be seen shortly on the walk. The clayrocks forming the roof to the coal contain fossil mussel* shells, suggesting that these clayrocks formed as mud on the bed of a lake or lagoon. This indicates that after the formation of peat (later the Yard Coal) the area was flooded and the peat buried by sediment. The sediment load eventually became great enough to convert the peat to coal.

Return to the road junction near the car park and head southwards, across the cattle grid, to walk down the Goyt valley. This

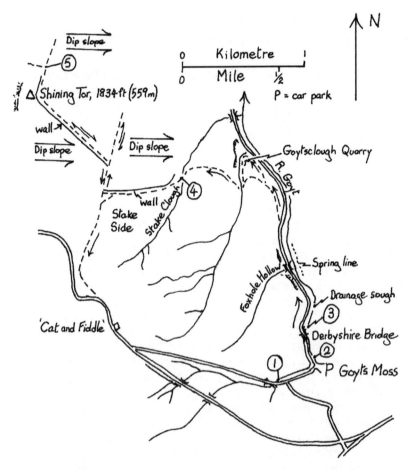

Figure 59: Sketch map of the Goyt's Moss - Shining Tor area.

section of road is one-way and such traffic as there is comes up the valley, which makes walking on it relatively safe. At certain times the road is closed to traffic altogether. Take care nevertheless!

Almost at the cattle grid (locality 2, Fig. 59) there is a slope of clayrock material, mostly loose, on the right-hand side. When freshly broken this material is dark in colour because of included organic matter. Only a small proportion of organic carbon is needed to make a rock very dark and at about 4% there is enough carbon to make a rock

Figure 60: Fault in roadside exposure, Goyt's Moss.

black. Once weathering has started the iron minerals present (mostly pyrite*, iron sulphide and siderite*, iron carbonate) are oxidised and hydrated to form iron oxides and hydroxides, responsible for the brown 'rusty' colours seen. About 30m below the cattle grid there is a small fault in the cliff to the right of the road, illustrated in Fig. 60. Continue down the road, noting that the stream on the left progressively cuts down into lower formations, forming waterfalls in passage over tougher sandstones.

At Derbyshire Bridge (locality 3, Fig. 59) leave the road to continue on the right (east) bank of the River Goyt and walk a few metres to a rock exposure. The lower part of the Yard Coal can be exposed here, but may be obscured by debris from above. The coal should be inspected to see the banding produced by different kinds of preservations of plant material. Identify the principal joint* direction, or 'cleat'. The coal rests on a seatearth*, with rootlets. Part of the seatearth forms a predominant band a short distance above the level of the river (look in loose blocks of sandstone for fossil plant debris).

Rejoin the road and continue down the valley. Just before a major tributary joins the River Goyt from the right a drainage tunnel (sough*, pronounced 'suff') will be seen just above stream level on the right. This sough was driven to drain the coal workings. Note that it passes through the sandstone below the level of the seam. Also note the cross-stratification* in the road opposite the sough. Downstream from the sough the valley is developed between steep sides, a testimony to the toughness of the Woodhead Hill Rock. At one point baskets filled with limestone chippings have been used to stabilise the ground near the road. Look across to the opposite (right) side of the valley to identify the spring line* at the base of the Woodhead Hill Rock (a similar situation is shown in Fig. 47). Water is able to penetrate through the sandstone (largely down joint* systems), but on meeting clayrocks or siltstones below, the water flow is blocked and diverted sideways to produce springs at the surface. Note the fresh vegetation established around the site of the spring. Just before reaching Foxhole Hollow on the left, look out for outcrops of sandstone just above the road. Here there are further good examples of cross-stratification*. This is a good place to observe the deep incision* of the River Goyt into the general land surface. Such a feature is common in the Peak District and surrounding areas.

Continue downstream, but watch for a signpost (indicating the directions to Goytsclough Quarry and Stake Side) at the start of a path which leaves the road on the left-hand side, heading obliquely up the hillside. Take this path which leads up to and along the edge of a wood to meet a fork. Take the right fork for Goytsclough Quarry. The view ahead, to the north, takes in Foxlow Edge, which is an excellent example of an escarpment*, with a steep scarp slope* (to the left) and a gentle dip slope* (to the right). The rocks here are folded into a downfold, or syncline*, known as the Goyt Syncline. Foxlow Edge is on the western limb of the syncline with dips to the east. The exposures of the Woodhead Hill Rock seen near the start of the walk were also on the western limb. Dip slopes on the far (eastern) side of the River Goyt result from a dip in the opposite direction. Therefore, the predominant slopes of the Goyt Valley coincide roughly with the dip of the rocks below.

The sandstone seen in the disused Goytsclough Quarry belongs to the Rough Rock (Fig. 3). Good examples of cross-stratification will be seen. There are also interesting carbonate concretions* which are intact and have not (yet) undergone the weathering which will cause decay of the binding calcite cement. Good examples can be seen in the quarry face from the top of a pile of quarry waste. Return to the road from the quarry and turn right onto the path signposted Stake Side and Shining Tor (route 5). Ascend the path and pass through the gate into a Forestry Commission wood towards a second signpost for Stake Side and Shining Tor.

The path now crosses a stream and climbs up the long dip slope (Stake Side) of the Rough Rock. Ascend to the crestline of Stake Side where there are good views, notably of Shutlingslow to the south-west. The top of Shutlingslow is capped by sandstone, a remnant of the Chatsworth Grit, isolated by erosion from adjacent outcrops. Such an isolated outcrop is known as an outlier*. At the signpost follow the direction for Stake Side and Shining Tor and continue, past the left turn for Shining Tor, along the crest with a wall to the left until an open view is had to the north, including Errwood Reservoir. The geological control of the landscape is very clear from here. Dip slopes indicate the form of the Goyt Syncline. The tough sandstones form all the ridges. Note, too, the general concordance of summit levels, suggesting that this whole area was once a raised plateau that has now been dissected by river erosion, a process that continues. Although the Goyt Valley happens to lie in a syncline it is important to realise that not all valleys of the Peak District are so located. The Todd Brook valley to the north-west, for instance, happens to lie on an anticline*! Return to the turn off for Shining Tor.

This path first descends the scarp slope of the Rough Rock then crosses on to the dip slope of the next sandstone down in the succession, which is the Chatsworth Grit (Fig. 3). Even though there are no rock exposures, the form of the topography allows an interpretation of what the rock structure is beneath. The summit of Shining Tor, at 1834ft (559m), together with a triangulation point, is reached via a stile and a very short detour. The views from this locality are superb. On clear days the Welsh hills can be seen to the west. To the north the escarpment of the Chatsworth Grit can be followed to Windgather Rocks. The outcrops of sandstone in the summit area reveal a coarse-grained sandstone with grains and pebbles of quartz* (glassy) and grains of feldspar* (pink). In places, the feldspar is being altered to a white kaolin clay, due to the action of acid rain and/or peat water. When the feldspar is completely converted to clay it is easily removed from the rock, which then appears pitted. Similar sandstone is characteristic of the Chatsworth Grit seen on Walk 5 on Millstone Edge. Return across the stile to the path and turn left (north) in the direction of Pym Chair. Near the point where the Lamaload path leaves to the left (locality 5, Fig. 59) there is much peat. Here the pieces of sandstone in contact with peat reveal feldspar in various states of decay.

Retrace steps to the crest of the Rough Rock then follow the signs to the 'Cat and Fiddle', which, at nearly 1,700 ft (510m) is the second highest pub in England, then continue to the car park at Goyts Moss.

Walk 14: Ashford-in-the-Water – Magpie Mine

'Black Marble' and Lead

Start of Walk: Car park in Ashford-in-the-Water (SK 194 698).

Maps:

   Topographical: :25 000 OS Explorer Map OL24, The Peak District. White Peak Area

   Geological: British Geological Survey Sheet SK16 Monyash. 1:50 000 Sheet 111, Buxton (Solid and Drift Edition)

Distance: 6½ miles (10km)

Refreshments: Nearby shops, cafés in Ashford-in-the-Water, toilets adjacent to car park.

From the car park walk to the road junction and green immediately to the west, then turn south to reach and cross the former pack-horse bridge, known as Sheepwash Bridge. This name relates to the practice of holding sheep in an enclosure on the down-stream side of the bridge prior to being washed in the river and sheared. More information about the bridge and the village is given on a plaque on the Ashford side of the bridge. At the A6, cross the road and turn right (west). On the way to the road junction ahead note an exposure, on the left, of limestone* beds alternating with clayrock* partings. Note that the limestones are not particularly dark in hue, an observation that will be commented on later.

At the road junction, leave the A6 by turning left up the road for Sheldon. In a few metres, opposite a Z-bend road sign, enter a small quarry, now much overgrown, and examine the quarry face developed in a rock sequence similar to that just seen by the A6. Thin dark limestones are seen to alternate so regularly with clayrock bands that the impression is given of masonry. The darkness of the limestone beds is due to included clay and organic matter. The rock takes a good polish, when it becomes jet black. Bands of it were worked here as 'Black Marble'* and it was used for decorative purposes. It was often inlaid with coloured stones. Material was extracted first from the quarry and then from underground galleries where it was worked by the 'pillar and stall'* method of mining, where the roof was supported by pillars of the rock and by pillars ('packs') of stonework. This was the Arrock Mine. Such abandoned workings are extremely dangerous and should never be entered without an experienced guide. 'Black Marble' was worked mainly between the late 18th and late 19th

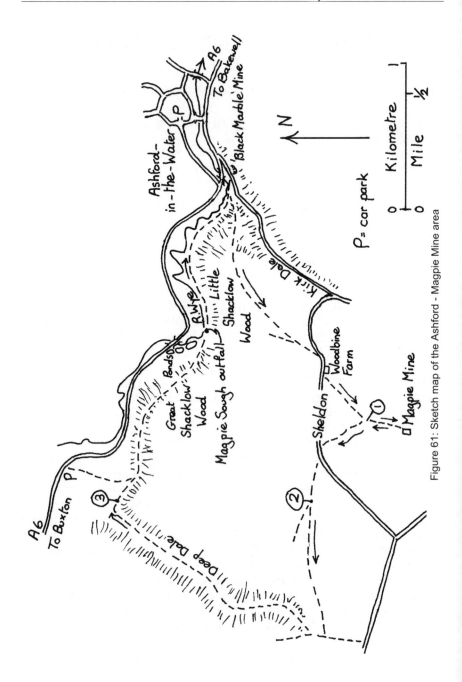

Figure 61: Sketch map of the Ashford - Magpie Mine area

century. There were several mines in the district in addition to the Arrock and the stone was polished at a mill only a few metres away from the Arrock Mine, on the opposite bank of the Wye. 'Marble'* is a term used by masons and stone workers for any soft rock that will take a good polish. To scientists the term 'marble' means a limestone that has been recrystallised by heat and/or pressure, so the Ashford rock, although a marble to the stone trade, is a limestone to science!

From the 'marble' quarry continue along the road in the direction of Sheldon, for about 100m then take the path leading off to the right. This path crosses through a gate, then divides. One fork continues to follow the line of the River Wye, and will be the route back at the end of the walk. Take the other (left) fork, to climb the hill up towards Little Shacklow Wood, passing a post with a yellow marker. Over to the left, below the telecommunications tower, there are good examples of terracettes* (good examples are seen later in the walk – see Fig. 62). Continue uphill bearing right past another yellow marker and later, a stile, note that on broken pieces of limestone the outer, weathered surfaces are much lighter than the fresh interiors. This suggests that the process of weathering causes the transfer of lime (calcium carbonate) from the interior to the outside of the rock. This would explain why the limestones seen in the outcrop by the A6 were relatively light in hue, whereas the same beds seen in the 'marble quarry' were much darker. The more the weathering, the lighter the limestone. One of the unfortunate characteristics of the Black Marble was this loss of blackness on weathering and the material is only suitable for indoor use.

As the path approaches Sheldon, a dry valley appears to the right (with terracettes*, see Fig. 62). Note that the limestone in the walls hereabouts is a mixture of dark and light limestone blocks, the latter often rich in crinoid* remains. The dark limestones apparently formed in relatively deep, and calm, water where mud could settle and mix with the future limestone on the sea floor. Such limestones are referred to as of 'basin' type, or as geologists would say, of 'basin facies'* the latter word indicating the total rock characteristics. The lighter limestones apparently formed in a marine shelf environment, under more turbulent environments where mud was unable to settle. Such limestones are referred to as belonging to a 'shelf facies'*.

At the road turn right towards the village of Sheldon, cross the top end of the dry valley, then just after the 30mph sign turn left along a footpath leading towards Magpie Mine. This path passes through stiles, one with splendid examples of shells and crinoids, before reaching a junction (locality 1, Fig. 61) of several paths and a signpost.

Turn left here, for the round chimney at the Mine. A stile on the way contains more crinoid remains.

Magpie Mine is the best preserved monument to the former lead mining industry in the Peak District. The site lies close to the intersection of several lead veins that were worked by a number of independent mines. Many bitter disputes arose, some leading to deaths, concerning mining rights where veins met or crossed. There are over 20 (covered) shafts on the site and care is required when walking around. Magpie has been worked, on and off, since at least the mid 18th century until closure in 1959.

The present headgear and associated winding equipment date from the most recent mining operations in the 1950s. There is a notice with details of the mine's history adjacent to the headgear. The shaft here (the Main Shaft) is 728ft (222m) deep, the lowest 47m being flooded The large stone building alongside the winding gear is the engine house where a Cornish beam engine was installed in 1869, replacing an earlier Newcomen-type engine. These engines were used to pump water from the workings to the surface. The high cost of coal led to construction, between 1873 and 1881, of an underground drainage tunnel, or 'sough'* (pronounced 'suff') which led from an intake 574ft (175m) down the shaft to the Wye valley, rather more than a mile away to the north. Its outfall is to be seen later in the walk. After construction of the sough, pumping was needed only to sough level. The square chimney seen on the site served an old winding engine, long since gone, but was then used for a later engine by extending the flue. A replica of a horse gin used for winding ore to the surface is also to be seen on the site. During the summer months be sure to look for the lead-tolerant Vernal Sandwort or Leadwort, *Minuartia verna*, on the tips (see Fig. 9).

From the round chimney (built for use with the pumping engines) return along the path towards Sheldon, crossing a field and going through a stile with a yellow arrow, in a general direction just west of north, to pass to the left of the village. The walls on the way are of interest because of their fossil content. The path reaches the road at a stile. Here turn left, away from the village, follow the road round a left bend and, in a few metres, turn off right at a path heading westwards towards Deep Dale. At the second stile, close to a power line post (locality 2, Fig. 61) take the left fork in the track which heads almost due west, crossing the fields and passing through a number of stiles, some of which incorporate worked and engraved sandstone blocks (derived, presumably, from a dismantled building or monument of some sort). The penultimate stile before reaching the path running down Deep Dale is made of limestone with magnificent crinoid remains.

Turn right at the path down Deep Dale (a dry valley*), pass old lead workings, then meet a dew pond. The need for a dew pond here is a powerful reminder of the water shortage problem in limestone areas during dry times in the year. Note the terracettes*, illustrated in Fig. 62, on the valley sides. Much of the stone in the walls is dark in hue, of basin facies. In places the limestone in the walls contains numerous, large productoid* brachiopod shells, often replaced by silica.

Towards the bottom of Deep Dale take the right fork to turn into the Wye valley, in the direction of Ashford-in-the-Water. Shortly after the fork (locality 3, Fig.61) the path crosses a surface of limestone rich in large productoid shells seen in horizontal section to appear like circles on the rock surface. Follow the yellow markers and signs to 'Ashford', passing meadows rich in wild flowers during the summer months. Ignore the track which leads off left to the car park on the nearby A6. The track now ascends into the lovely Great Shacklow Wood, with examples of trees with curved trunks (see Fig. 51) indicating unstable ground. The path shortly descends to the river and reaches the outfall of the Magpie Sough. It then continues to meet

Figure 62: Terracettes, Deep Dale.

the Sheldon-Ashford road to complete the circuit. Return to Ashford-in-the-Water and the car park.

The care and maintenance of the surface buildings at Magpie Mine is in the hands of the Peak District Mines Historical Society. Further information about Magpie Mine and lead mining in general in the Peak District, is available at the Peak District Mining Museum, Matlock Bath. A good account of Magpie Mine is given in Ford and Rieuwert's *Lead Mining in the Peak District.*

Walk 15: Tegg's Nose

Sandstone and Sandstone Quarries

Start of Walk: Tegg's Nose Country Park. Car park (SJ 950 733)

Maps:

Topographical: 1:25 000 OS Explorer Map OL 24, The Peak District. White Peak Area

Geological: British Geological Survey 1:50 000 Sheet 110, Macclesfield (Solid Edition and Drift Edition)

Distance: 2 miles (3km)

Refreshments: Pubs and cafés in Macclesfield, picnic area and toilets adjacent to car park.

Enter the Visitor Centre and examine the sandstone walls. Lamination* (small scale stratification) is very clear in most of the building blocks. This lamination is produced by the presence of (darker) clay-rich or mica-rich layers between (lighter) layers of sandstone. Fossil ripple structures in section are also revealed by the presence of clay and mica layers (in the form of 'ripple lamination'*). Of special interest here are funnel-shaped structures in the lamination, shown in Fig. 64. These structures are known as escape shafts* and were produced by the action of 'mussel'* shells, which had to 'escape' upwards when deposition of sediment threatened burial, as in Fig. 65. As the mussels moved upwards the sediment fell in behind them, so that the structures formed as upward-opening funnels, rather like a stack of ice-cream cones. Escape shafts are therefore an indicator as to which way is 'top' of a sediment layer. Examination of the escape shafts in the walls of the Visitor Centre shows that many of the building blocks were placed upside down! The presence of escape shafts is a measure of how rapidly some of these sediments accumulated. On the floor of the Visitor Centre artificial stone flags have been used. They have been moulded to look like flags with parting lineation* and close inspection soon shows that the patterns on the flags repeat! These artificial flags have been used outside the Centre, too. The roof of the Centre is made of slate.

In the car park immediately adjacent to the Visitor Centre are raised block displays illustrating The Gritstone Trail, Tegg's Trail, Macclesfield Forest and Shutlingslow Summit (locality 1, Fig. 63). Shutlingslow is located in the distance to the south. The summit of this hill is composed of a cap of sandstone (the Chatsworth Grit, see

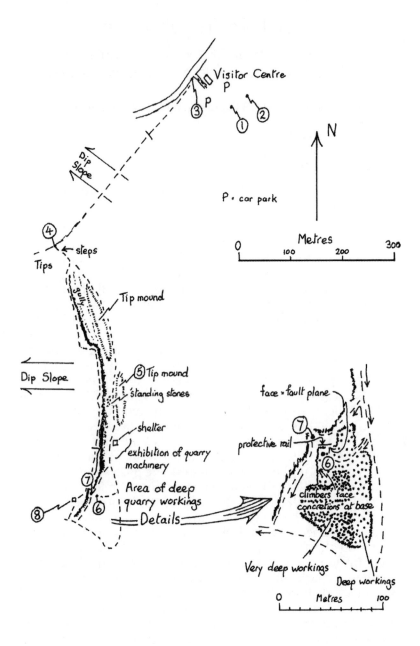

Figure 63: Sketch map of the Tegg's Nose area.

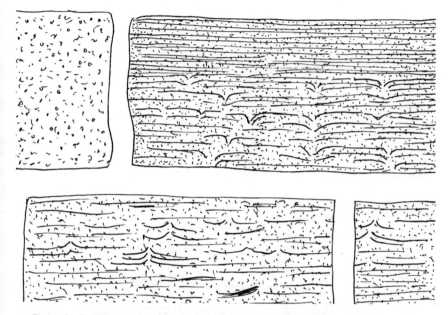

Figure 64: Building stones at the Visitor Centre, Tegg's Nose, with 'escape' structures produced by 'mussel' shells when alive. The top right block is the 'right way up', the lower two blocks are 'upside down'. See text.

Fig. 3) which is the last remnant of what was once a continuous sheet of sandstone. Such residual masses, now detached from the main outcrop, are known as outliers*. Adjacent to the displays there are four stone steps. One of these shows a good example of parting lineation (see Fig. 12b) with its characteristic 'grain'. Also in close proximity is a sandstone block containing pebbles of clayrock*, or cavities from which such pebbles have been removed. Rock of this type is known as mudflake conglomerate*. At the north-east corner of this car park (locality 2, Fig. 63) there is a seat, adjacent to which is a pile of sandstone blocks, with more examples of mudflake conglomerate.

Leave the Visitor Centre and walk to the road, where there is a sign for 'Gritstone Trail' and 'To the Country Park'. There is a row of four boulders by the path near the sign (locality 3, Fig. 63). The outermost boulders of the row are composed of rock unlike the local rocks as seen in quarries and natural outcrops. This rock is a granite*, with large interlocking grains of quartz* (glassy) and feldspar* (altering to kaolin clay*). The granite can be identified as the Eskdale Granite of the Lake District and it arrived in this area by ice transport during the

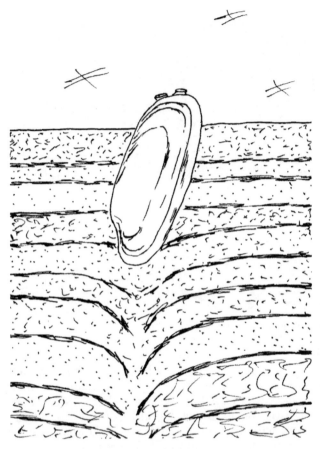

last cold phase of the Pleistocene* glaciation. Specimens of this granite, together with other Lake District and southern Scottish rocks are to be found in abundance in the glacial deposits of the district. A short distance along the path are four more boulders, one of them composed of Eskdale Granite. Pass through a stile and continue along the path. There is now a good view of the Cheshire Plain. Note the stark contrast between the scenery there,

Figure 65: 'Mussel' escaping the effects of burial by sedimentation. Note sediment deformation below in the form of an 'escape' trail. Water above.

developed on the softer rocks of the New Red Sandstone* (Permo-Triassic* in age), and the scenery of the immediate area developed on the tougher rocks of the Carboniferous* (about 300 million years in age). A fault*, the Red Rock Fault, separates the two areas. The rocks of the Cheshire Plain are on the downthrown* side of the fault, Tegg's Nose is on the upthrown* side. The rocks of the Cheshire Plain are underlain at depth by Carboniferous rocks, which have been reached in boreholes. Note the even slope of the ground in

Figure 66: Quarry face at Tegg's Nose. Note the cross-stratification half-way up the face suggesting current flow from left to right.

the vicinity of the track. This is a surface formed by a sloping bed of sandstone beneath. Such a surface is known as a dip slope*.

At the second stile (locality 4, Fig. 63) turn left, climb up some rough steps to the main path, following yellow arrows. There are good views across Macclesfield Forest to the left, including the outlier of Chatsworth Grit forming the summit of Shutlingslow.

At the quarry face it is possible to climb up a bank (locality 5, Fig. 63) to get a good view of the features in the face. The rock formation here belongs to the upper part of the Chatsworth Grit (see Fig. 3) and consists of thin sandstones alternating with thin siltstone* and clayrock beds. Approximately half way up this face there is a bed with cross-stratification*, shown in Fig. 66 (see also Fig. 26). This rock succession is interpreted as a lagoon deposit where deposition of muds and silt were interrupted occasionally by the arrival of river-transported sands which were spread across the floor of the lagoon as 'splays'. Such deposits were probably related to flood events in the rivers flowing into the lagoon.

In front of the quarry face is a splendid display, with explanatory notices, of some of the machinery that was once used in the working

of quarries such as this one. There is a frame saw* (described here by the unusual name of 'swing saw') used for slicing sandstone blocks into flags, a crane, a jaw crusher. There is also a display of the kind of products made, including setts* (shaped blocks for use in road surfaces), flags, gate posts, and building blocks. In front of a stone shelter there is a large (1m x 1.5m) rectangular slab, laid horizontally on the ground, showing superb parting lineation*.

Figure 67: Slickensides, the polishing and scouring caused by faulting in rocks. The face depicted moved to the bottom left relative to the observer.

Beyond the exhibits take the left fork in the path (following the yellow markers) and walk about 50m to gain a good view into a deep excavation in the quarry. The rocks here are dominated by thick beds of sandstone with a dip* of about 20° to the west. Within the sandstone beds are localised bodies of highly weathered rock in carbonate concretions*, darker in colour than the surrounding rock. They will be examined at close quarters, shortly. On the side of the path, away from the quarry, there are large sandstone blocks, some with good examples of fossil ripple marks.

Retrace steps towards the machinery exhibit and in a few metres turn left down a steep track into the deep quarry workings. The path leads to a point (locality 6, Fig. 63) close to the junction of two quarry walls. The north-south face, used by rock-climbers, is formed by a joint* plane, and contains the carbonate concretions, one of which can be examined closely. Notice how the cement has been attacked making the sandstone crumbly and friable. The other face is formed by a fault plane and the characteristic polishing and scoring features (slickensides*) are well displayed, as shown in Fig. 67. There is another concretion here, also a good display of cross-stratification* (suggesting current flow towards the west).

Retrace steps out of the deep working and walk back towards the machinery exhibits. Just before reaching them, at the path junction, turn left to walk towards an extension of the quarry face, and to the protective wooden fence (locality 7, Fig. 63) at the edge of the deep quarry workings. There is a good view from here of the face used by the rock climbers. In the vicinity of the fence, on the side of the path away from the deep workings, at the foot of the quarry face, are loose blocks of sandstone, some with bedding plane surfaces rich in mica*, others with plant remains – see Fig. 68. There are also presumed 'mussel' inpressions here (see Fig. 12c), seen on bedding planes, rather than in cross-section as they were in the Visitor Centre). These impressions are all about the same size, suggesting that the culprits

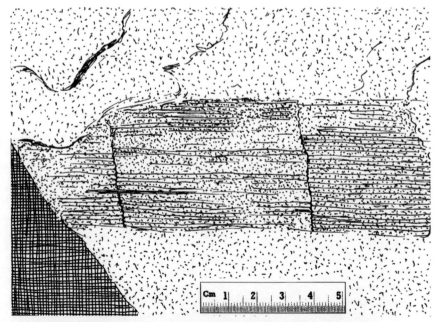

Figure 68: Fossil plant in sandstone, the horsetail Calamites, Tegg's Nose.

were all about the same age (no 'babies') and possibly represent one generation. Note the alternation of sandstones and siltstones in the quarry face, also the sets of joints* (see Fig. 5) which control the pattern of fracturing.

Continue along the path at the base of the quarry face to meet a roadway. Turn right here, then right again to climb up to a viewpoint (locality 8, Fig. 63) over the Cheshire Plain. There is a panoramic display board here. Continue along the ridge. The first stone wall reached has a circular seat built into it with direction indicator blocks embedded at intervals all around the top of the wall. Nearby there are good views down into the quarry and machinery display below.

The route back to the Visitor Centre is straightforward.

Walk 16: Tideswell Dale – Miller's Dale

Limestones and Lavas

Start of Walk: Tideswell Picnic Area car park (SK 153 743)

Maps:

 Topographical: 1:25 000 OS Explorer OL24, The Peak District. White Peak Area

 Geological: British Geological Survey 1:50 000 Sheet 111, Buxton (Solid and Drift Edition)

Distance: 5½ miles (9km)

Refreshments: in Tideswell and Miller's Dale. Toilets and picnic area adjacent to car park.

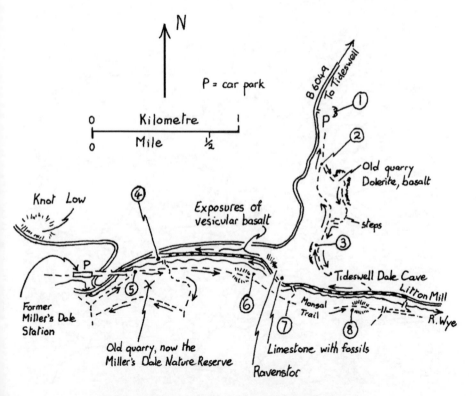

Figure 69: Sketch map of the Tideswell - Miller's Dale area.

Figure 70: Spheroidal weathering in dolerite, Tideswell Dale.

In the picnic area, opposite to the road entrance, is a disused quarry (locality 1, Fig.69). The quarry face consists of dolerite*. This rock is relatively rich in iron and so weathers to produce the brown 'rust' colours seen here. This quarry face shows a good example of spheroidal weathering* in which relatively fresh spherical or ovoid masses of rock are enclosed by rotten rock, shown in Fig. 70. Chemical weathering has progressed down joint planes and along horizontal fractures to isolate the centres of relatively fresh rock.

Walk down the Dale to reach a gate and stile. Immediately beyond the stile (locality 2, Fig. 69) leave the main path and turn left up a track, past limestone* outcrops, to a stile leading into a large disused dolerite quarry (a picnic site). This dolerite is interpreted as a sill*, known as the Tideswell Sill. More spheroidal weathering is to be seen here. Cross the stile and walk north-north-east for about 25 metres to reach a group of three small boulders, one of which shows relatively unweathered rock, very dark in hue and with a fine-grain size. Such material is identified as basalt*, normally produced as lava. A lava flow is recorded in this quarry and may have been the source of this specimen. Note the colour of the weathered surface, where oxidation and hydration have altered the iron in the rock to oxides and hydroxides, thereby generating the typical 'rusty' colours. Continue in the same direction to the boundary fence of the picnic area. Another boulder, just on the far side of the fence also exhibits a fresh face, very dark in hue, but is much coarser in grain size, justifying the term dolerite. Nearby are numerous rounded masses, like cannon balls, of similar material and these represent the cores produced by spheroidal weathering. Continue round the fence in the direction of the main quarry face to reach a large boulder on the picnic side of the fence. This boulder is composed of weathered doleritic material but fractures and cavities are filled by the mineral calcite*. The nearby signpost indicates the direction of a concessionary footpath, which should be taken. Note the deep gully to the right, which once exposed the base of the dolerite sill. The path continues southwards, down steps, back to the floor of Tideswell Dale. Cross the stream and turn left to continue down the dale. Above, to the right, are well-bedded limestones (locality 3, Fig. 69), with clay bands separating individual limestone beds. Lower down the dale, just before reaching Miller's Dale, the entrance to Tideswell Dale Cave will be seen, often nearly hidden by vegetation, on the left of the footpath.

At the junction of Tideswell Dale with Miller's Dale examine the limestone cliff by the roadside. The limestone strata here are sometimes massive indicating that they are relatively pure and lack a significant clay content, but may also appear rubbly, like lumpy porridge, where concentrations of clay 'impurity' are in the process of being removed (for another example, see Fig. 33). There appears to be a cyclic development in that rubbly limestones change progressively upwards into more massive limestones, then there is a return, abruptly, to rubbly beds and the sequence starts again. Continue along the (metalled) road, past the entrance to Ravenstor Youth Hostel, past a footbridge over the River Wye and into a right-hand bend in the road. The limestone here contains a shell bed, well seen in joint* faces, with large productoid brachiopods* and crinoids*. Some of the brachiopods show stacking*, an indicator of deposition under turbulent conditions. Round the bend the impressive cliff of Ravenstor will be seen, frequented by rock climbers. This cliff is composed of limestone, but with a basalt lava flow (with an irregular top) at the base. The basalt is best seen in roadside exposures further to the west. Here it can be seen in various states of weathering. It contains gas bubbles (so is 'vesicular'*) and in places the bubbles have been filled with mineral material, such as calcite. Continue along the road and note the position of a spring on the right-hand side of the road, shortly before reaching the road junction at the Anglers Rest pub. This spring is developed at the junction of the limestone (above) and the lava (below), suggesting that the lava is acting like a damp-proof course and is forcing out the water that has passed down through the limestone above.

Just before the road junction is reached there is a water wheel on the left-hand side of the road (locality 4, Fig. 69), at the site of the former Miller's Dale Mill (where there is an interesting explanatory notice). From the mill site take the footpath which crosses the River Wye, reaches a sign for 'Monsal Trail' and 'Priestcliffe', passes outcrops of rubbly limestone, and arrives at an abandoned railway track, the Monsal Trail. Cross over the track and enter the Miller's Dale Nature Reserve, a Site of Special Scientific Interest (SSSI) and once a major quarry until a crack appeared above the quarry face in 1930 and forced closure. The presence of a lava flow (the Upper Miller's Dale Lava) directly beneath this limestone is thought to be connected with the instability. An informative notice, with map, detailed history and notes on the wildlife, is placed at the entrance to the Reserve. Ascend the path to the level of the quarry floor and turn right along a more or less level path at the edge of the quarry workings. There is a good view from here, to the north-west, of Knot Low, a hill capped with basalt lava. At the far end of the quarry track there are close views of the disused quarry faces. Note the jointing* as well as bedding*. The path shortly meets a trail leading back to Miller's Dale down a steep slope. Take this path and look for outcrops of the lava which might be responsible for the quarry closure. This lava flow is to be seen again, later in the walk. Descend further, then take a right fork which leads to the Monsal Trail and lime kilns (locality 5, Fig. 69), immediately to the east of the impressive viaducts which once carried the railway over the river. There are notices here with details about the kilns and the Miller's Dale Nature Reserve, respectively. The kilns closed down in 1930 when the quarry ceased to operate. Walk along the railway track eastwards, to return to the original entry point to the Reserve.

Continue eastwards along the Monsal Trail to a deep cutting on a slight right bend. At the far end of the cutting look for fossils in the limestone on the left side (locality 6, Fig. 69). There are interesting brachiopods to see here. The bedding on the right-hand side of the cutting will be seen to dip very gently down towards the east, so that progress along the Monsal Trail brings in progressively younger beds. Once beyond the cutting, walk to the left to gain a superb view of the River Wye below and the cliff of Ravenstor on the far bank. The Trail crosses a path (from Priestcliff to Ravenstor) at locality 7, Fig. 69. Here the view to the north-east across the Wye valley shows an escarpment* of limestone on the skyline, also outcrops, all indicating a gentle dip* to the east. Shortly, the Monsal Trail curves to the right to enter another high cutting, with a bridge shortly beyond. In the cutting, watch out for exposures of the Upper Miller's Dale Lava on the right (locality 8, Fig. 69). The presence of this lava here is the consequence of the easterly dip bringing down progressively younger beds. The exposure of the lava is rather overgrown, but it is possible to locate the point at which the lava stopped flowing! The overlying limestones are draped over the lava front (see adjacent notice for a more detailed description).

Further along the cutting there are good exposures of the limestone, with partings of clayrock* and nodules of chert*. Note the jointing, one set is especially well-developed. Fossils will also be seen in the limestone. A short distance beyond the footbridge take the path leading off to the left, over limestone 'steps' with large brachiopod fossils, and across a footbridge to Litton Mill. This part of the route forms part of the Monsal Dale walk. At Litton Mill turn left, then back up Tideswell Dale. Ignore the bridge crossed earlier, and continue straight up Tideswell Dale to the car park.

Walk 17: Rowarth – Cown Edge

Faults, Folds and Landslips

Start of Walk: Car park at Rowarth (SK 010 892)

Maps:
   Topographical: 1:25 000 OS Explorer Map: OL1, The Peak District. Dark
   Peak Area
   Geological: British Geological Survey 1:50 000 Sheet 99,
   Chapel-en-le-Frith (Solid Edition and Drift Edition)

Distance: 4 miles (6.5km)

Refreshments: Nearby pub in Rowarth

From the car park walk north-eastwards into the village of Rowarth
(noting the Drinkwater Buildings, 1812, on the left), continue past the
road junction, then turn left at the footpath sign, for Cown Edge, after
the last house ('Poplar Farm') on the left. This path climbs steadily at
first, northwards, up a slope formed on an inclined sandstone*
surface (largely hidden beneath the soil but exposed in small outcrops
best seen in old quarry workings beyond the second stile (locality 1,
Fig. 71). Such a slope is known as a dip slope*.Continue up the hill,
cross a path junction at a stile, then, as the gradient slackens and the
village of Rowarth is about to 'disappear', stop to enjoy the view to the
south. Note the control of the scenery by the presence of the tough
sandstones, folded into a downfold, or sycline – the Goyt Syncline, Fig.
72.

   Continue the walk, now up a reduced slope, heading northwards.
Soon a wall appears ahead with a wooden stile, locality 2, Fig. 71. Pass
through the stile, then take the right fork to keep on high ground
across the moor – which, as will be seen shortly, is another dip slope.
However, note that the slopes now dip west, not south, and indicate
that a major structural boundary has been crossed since leaving
Rowarth. There are good views from here to the west, across the
Lancashire-Cheshire plain and to Manchester and its environs. Note
the contrast between the flatness of the plain and the topography of
the immediate surroundings. The plain is underlain by the relatively
'soft' rocks of the Permo-Trias*, the immediate ground by the tough
rocks of the Carboniferous*. The two areas are separated by a major
fault, the Red Rock Fault. The walk continues past another wall with
stile and gate. Far Slack will be seen to the north-west. The path
continues with Far Slack to the left and reaches a wall junction and

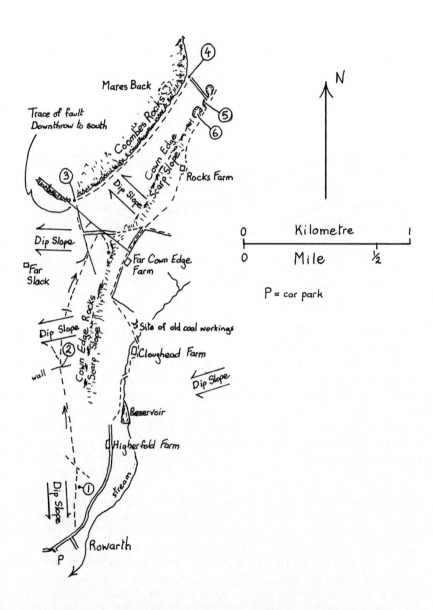

Figure 71: Sketch map of the Cown Edge area.

Figure 72: View of Lantern Pike from above Rowarth.

stile. From here there is a view to the north of the trace of a fault, beyond which the ground has been raised – see Fig. 73. The displacement of this fault increases to the west. Walk to the line of the fault and note that it runs into a gully through Cown Edge Rocks to the east. Even small faults cause shattering of tough rocks like sandstone, and the shattered rock is easily removed by erosion. Walk eastwards along the edge of the gully to a point above Far Cown Edge Farm, for a good view along Cown Edge to the north. Cown Edge is a scarp slope*. The sandstone exposed in the crags is the Rough Rock which dips gently at about 5° in a westerly direction, forming the dip slope.

Return to the gully, cross the stile on to the roadway and walk down towards the west. At the next stile turn right, along a wall to cross the line of the fault and on to the upthrown side to reach a superb viewpoint (locality 3, Fig. 71) over Coombes Rocks, a splendid example of a landslip, Fig. 73. Note that the southern limit of the landslip is determined by the fault just crossed. Conditions are ideal here for landslip formation. The tough sandstone at the top of the landslip is the Rough Rock. Beneath the sandstone the rock succession is dominated by rocks rich in clayrocks* and siltstones*, with relatively little strength. The entire sequence tilts (dips) into the

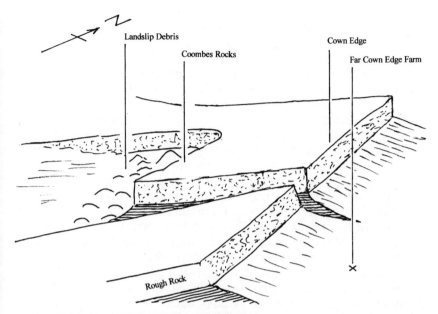

Figure 73: Model to illustrate the type of faulting that has occurred in the vicinity of the Coombes Rocks landslip.

landslip area. Dating, by pollen analysis, has shown the slip to have been active more than 8,000 years ago, shortly after the end of the last (Devensian) glaciation. Now walk along the path between the landslip edge and the fence. Note the feature of the Mare's Back below in the landslip area. Eventually a pine wood is reached on the right. Just beyond the northern limit of this wood take the second of the two stiles (locality 4, Fig. 71) through the fence, and walk up the roadway leading south-westwards away from the landslip and into an area of small quarries on Cown Edge. At the end of the roadway turn right into the small working immediately adjacent (locality 5, Fig. 71).

The sandstone in this quarry is coarse-grained, with quartz* pebbles, often in bands. The sandstone contains grains of feldspar*, many quite conspicuous because they have been weathered and so are white due to the development of kaolin* clay as a breakdown product. Cross-stratification* and carbonate concretions* are to be seen. Walk to the next quarry (locality 6, Fig. 71) a few metres to the south-east, where a solitary gate stands with no fence or wall on either side. In this quarry, near the entrance on the left, there are small concretions about the size and shape of tennis balls (for similar examples, see Fig. 20). Splendid examples of larger concretions are to be seen in the main quarry faces. Note the jointing* here, too. Return to the path and head down for Rocks Farm, with good views of the Goyt Syncline in the distance. Pass to the left of Rocks Farm (good signs) and continue in the direction of Rowarth. Note that over to the left (south-east) there is a dip slope, developed on the next sandstone beneath the Rough Rock (Chatsworth Grit, see Fig. 3). As Far Cown Edge comes into view, walk to join a farm track to pass the farm on the right. Once past the farm buildings look for the continuation of the path adjacent to a caravan, then head downslope keeping to a wall on the left. At the end of the wall there is a stile, beyond which the path turns towards the south-east for Cloughead Farm. As the farm is approached there are old coal workings to the left of the path.

A coal seam, the Simmondley Coal (see Fig. 3), about 0.75m thick, was worked here. The tips contain fragments of coal, together with fragments of black (carbon-rich) clayrocks which formed the roof to the coal seam. Stepping stones are provided to take the walker across the stream at Cloughead Farm. Walk round the farm to pass in front of the buildings to continue (past stables) alongside the stream. In a few metres there is a footbridge over the stream and the path then continues on the right bank to pass above a reservoir and on to Higherfold Farm (note the sandstone roof flags) and Rowarth.

Walk 18: Rowarth – Lantern Pike

Rocks and Topography

Start of Walk: Car park at Rowarth (SK 010 892)

Maps:

Topographical: 1:25 000 OS Explorer Map: OL1, The Peak District. Dark Peak Area

Geological: British Geological Survey 1:50 000 Sheet 99, Chapel-en-le-Frith (Solid Edition and Drift Edition)

Distance: 4¼ miles (7km)

Refreshments: Nearby pub in Rowarth

From the car park, walk eastwards into the village, then turn right at the road junction. At the telephone box, turn left and follow a delightful path above the stream. Note the outcrops of sandstone* in the stream. The path slowly converges on the stream and it is possible to walk over the bedding planes of the sandstone. Note that the dip* is to the south-west. Cross the stream by the ford and follow the road up the hill to and beyond Lower Harthill Farm. As the buildings of Higher Harthill Farm are approached take the path leading off to the left and steeply up on to a low ridge. Follow the path until a point (locality 1, Fig. 74) is reached above the buildings of Higher Harthill, noting, on the way, exposures of sandstone to the left of the path. These sandstones dip to the south and indicate that the slope of the ground around and below the farm comprise a dip slope*, i.e. the slope is formed by a bed of sandstone only a short distance beneath the soil. Look at the landscape beyond. The form of Lantern Pike and its continuation to the right (west) is controlled by a major downfold (syncline*) in the rocks, the Goyt Syncline. This syncline is tilted (plunges*) to the south so that the different beds in the limbs of the fold are closed around the end of the structure, rather like the rims in a stack of saucers. Harthill is one of the 'saucer' rims in the stack.

Continue eastwards towards Matleymoor Farm. At the stile (locality 2, Fig. 74) immediately in front of the farm there is a block of ganister* (silica-rich fossil soil), in this case with a fossilised root structure, *Stigmaria* – see Fig. 4b. Turn right at the road junction and look for another block of ganister (this time with fossil rootlets, see Fig. 4a) in the wall at the turn. Walk to the junction of paths adjacent to Blackshaw Farm. From here follow the path leading south-eastwards towards Lantern Pike. This path leads into a short

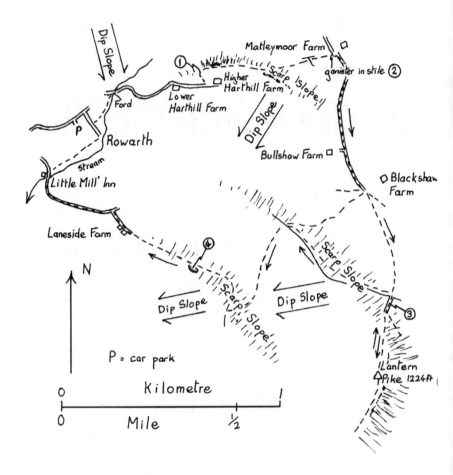

Figure 74: Sketch map of the Rowarth - Lantern Pike area.

section of roadway (locality 3, Fig. 74) flanked by stone walls. At the southern (far) end of this roadway follow the path which turns off to the right and leads to the summit of Lantern Pike at 1224 ft (373m), formed of sandstone (Rough Rock, see Fig. 3). There is a superlative view from here. Below, to the right, is Hayfield, flanked behind by a dip slope* of the Upper Kinderscout Grit, illustrated in Fig. 75. This dip slope has been incised* by the River Kinder. On the skyline to the east is the plateau of Kinder Scout, composed of the virtually flat Lower Kinderscout Grit (see Fig. 3), and containing the highest point

Figure 75: Hayfield and the gorge cut by the River Kinder through the dip slope of Kinderscout Grit behind.

of the Peak District at 2087 feet (636m). To the south is Chinley Churn with several ridges marking the outcrops of sandstones, here all on the eastern limb of the Goyt Syncline – see Fig. 76. To the north is Cown Edge, a splendid escarpment, seen on Walk 17. To the west the trigonometric point will be seen to rest on a geologically higher bed of sandstone, the Woodhead Hill Rock (elsewhere known as the Crawshaw Sandstone, see Fig. 3). The adjacent monument is also located on the outcrop of this sandstone.

From the summit of Lantern Pike retrace steps to locality 3, then turn left. Walk north-westwards, following the path along a scarp slope. This path meets a roadway and a left turn should be made (to the south-west) Follow this road to a T-junction (outcrops of sandstone, the Woodhead Hill Rock, in the road) and turn right in the direction of Rowarth. A small quarry (locality 4, Fig. 74) is soon reached on the left side of this road. The sandstone here is again the Woodhead Hill Rock. This location is close to the axis of the Goyt Syncline and the dip of about 10° towards the south is a measure of the plunge of the syncline. This plunge reverses in Chinley Churn so that the entire structure of the Goyt Syncline is shaped rather like a

Figure 76: Ridges formed by the presence of tough sandstones ('grits') on the eastern limb of the Goyt Syncline, above Birch Vale.

canoe. There are carbonate concretions* here, also examples of cross-stratification*. Continue along the road, across more exposures of the Woodhead Hill Rock to walk 'down' the rock succession, from the Woodhead Hill Rock, on to underlying softer clayrocks* and siltstones*. A number of Glacial erratics*, derived from local Boulder Clay*, are to be seen along this roadway, notably specimens of volcanic rocks which are very tough, are dark when fresh but develop a white skin on the surface when weathered. These rocks include lavas and tuffs* (consolidated ashes) and are identical in range of rock type with the Borrowdale Volcanic Group of rocks in the Lake District. This indicates that the ice which reached this area included some which had come from the Lake District. Continue to Rowarth at the Little Mill Inn. Here the Rough Rock is exposed in the stream bed adjacent to the water wheel. Walk on to the car park.

Glossary of Terms

Absolute Age

Age as measured in years or millions of years. To be distinguished from *relative* time where an object or event is older or younger than some other object or event.

Adit

An access tunnel or roadway, horizontal or inclined, leading to mine workings from the surface.

Anticline

An upfold in sedimentary rocks where the older rocks form the core. An example is the Todd Brook Anticline, see Fig. 6A. See 'Syncline'*.

Apron reef

Poorly-bedded limestone, with stromatolites*, corals and other fossils but lacking evidence of a skeletal binding structure. Occur along the edge of shelf areas of limestone deposition.

Barite or baryte

High density mineral, barium sulphate, $BaSO_4$. Used in the preparation of drilling mud, paint manufacture and as a filler for 'quality' paper.

Basalt

The most commonly encountered lava. Generally very dark, but weathers to various shades of brown due to the relatively high iron content.

Basin facies

The term 'facies'* indicates the sum of the features of a rock. 'Basin facies' refers to rocks, which on their features, are interpreted as having been deposited in deeper water regions.

Bedding

Rock layers.

Bell pits

Shallow shafts sunk to mineral beds, usually coal. Each shaft has a small area of workings at its base. On abandonment, collapse usually takes place to produce a hollow in the ground at the surface. See Fig. 44.

Black Marble

A limestone with an organic-rich clay 'impurity'. Such limestones generally take a good polish and are referred to as 'marbles' by the building trade. However the term 'marble', in its scientific usage, refs refers to a limestone which has been recrystallised by heat and/or pressure.

Blue John
A rare, banded variety of the mineral fluorite. Radiation is probably involved in the development of Blue John. For more details see description of Walk 2.

Boulder Clay or 'till'
A mix of clay and boulders deposited by an ice sheet or glacier.

Brachiopods
A group of marine invertebrates where the soft tissues are enclosed by two valves, generally not mirror images of each other. They were dominant on the sea floors of Carboniferous age, but are very uncommon today. They have been replaced by the Bivalves group of the molluscs. Most brachiopods were biconvex in form. See 'Productoid brachiopods*.

Brassington Formation
Sediments of Miocene* and Pliocene* age preserved in hollows of the Carboniferous Limestone in the southern part of the Peak District.

Breccia
(pronounced 'bretchia') Rock composed of angular rock fragments set in a finer-grained matrix. Formed either by rock fracturing in the vicinity of a fault (then a 'fault breccia') or by deposition as scree material.

Calcite
A mineral, calcium carbonate, $CaCO_3$. Soft (easily scratched by a steel blade). Three well-developed mineral cleavages*. The main component of limestone.

Carbonate concretions
Localised patches of sandstone cemented by calcite, the surrounding sandstone being cemented with silica*. On weathering the calcite cement is removed by solution and the sand grains released to leave a cavity. See Figs. 20, 27.

Carboniferous
A geological **Period** of time dating from 360 to 286 million years ago, also the **System** of rocks that were formed during that time (see Fig. 2).

Chalcopyrite
An important copper ore mineral, copper iron sulphide, $CuFeS_2$. Golden-yellow, brassy.

Chalk
A poorly cemented, soft limestone characteristic of the late Cretaceous Period, dating from 90 to 65 million years ago.

Chert
Rock composed of minute quartz crystals. Extremely tough. Occurs as bands or nodules in a variety of host rocks, especially limestones. Identical to flint.

Clayrock
Sedimentary rock composed essentially of clay minerals or clay-sized particles. Formerly known as 'shale' or 'mudstone'.

Clints
Upstanding blocks on a solution surface of limestone. Clints are separated from one another by channels (widened joints*) known as grikes.

Coal Measures
The upper part of the Upper Carboniferous succession in Britain, relatively rich in coal seams, not so rich in sandstones. However, the term 'Coal Measures' has now largely been replaced by 'Westphalian'*. See Fig. 2.

Concretions
Patches or nodules of sedimentary rock with a cement different from that of the surrounding rock. Concretion cements are usually silica, calcite* or siderite*.

Conglomerate
Sedimentary rock composed of rounded pebbles in a finer-grained matrix of sand or silt. Contrast with breccia*.

Corals
A group of marine, bottom-dwelling organisms which build a skeleton of calcium carbonate and may be colonial or solitary. They date from the Ordovician Period (505 to 438 million years ago, see Fig. 2). The Carboniferous corals are not closely related to modern corals.

Cross-stratification
An oblique stratification within individual beds of sandstone. Formed by deposition of sediment on the sloping down-current surface of a sandbank, or similar structure. The dip* of the cross-stratification provides evidence about the current flow direction at the time of formation. This structure is developed on a small scale as cross-lamination* in ripple structures. See Fig. 26.

Cretaceous

A geological Period of time, or System of rocks, dating from about 144 to 65 million years ago. See Fig. 2.

Crinoids

A group of marine animals, related to modern sea urchins and starfish (echinoderms), and which were important in the early part of the geological fossil record, including the Carboniferous, but are rare today. The Carboniferous crinoids, or sea lilies (a strange name for a group of animals), were attached to the sea floor by an anchor-type of structure and had a stem, typically about 0.3m long and a centimetre or so in width, made of stem columnals ('ossicles'), each with a hole in the centre, looking like 'Polo' mints. On top of the stem was the calyx, or cup, containing the bulk of the soft tissues and an arrangement of arms for collecting food. See Fig. 4h.

Crinoidal limestone

Limestone rich in crinoid* material, usually lengths of stem or stem ossicles.

Curved tree trunks

Tilting of young trees by soil movement downslope is 'corrected' by growth to produce the curvature of tree trunks on steep slopes. As trees become more established with extensive root systems the tilting ceases. See Fig. 51.

Cyanobacteria (or Blue-green Algae)

Organisms related to bacteria, but with chlorophyll, and which live in fresh waters or the sea. Tolerant of extreme conditions, including high temperatures. Form structures known as stromatolites* which are known from rocks 3400 million years in age. Stromatolites occur in the apron-reef limestones of the Peak District, See Fig. 37.

Devensian

The last of the Pleistocene* Glaciations. Commenced about 70,000 years ago and ended about 10,000 years ago.

Dinantian

The Lower (or Early) Carboniferous. See Fig. 2.

Dip

The tilt of rock strata or other geological feature. Measured in terms of angle from the horizontal, and in terms of direction.

Dip slope

Hillside developed on what is more or less the top surface of a tough rock layer or stratum. Dip slopes should be distinguished from scarp slopes*, see Fig. 42.

Dolerite
An igneous* rock with the composition of basalt* but with a coarser grain size.

Dolomite
A rock-forming mineral, calcium magnesium carbonate, $CaMg(CO_3)_2$. Rocks composed of the mineral dolomite are often also called 'dolomite' but should be distinguished by the term 'dolostone'. Many limestones undergo alteration by the addition of magnesium in the process of dolomitisation.

Dolomitisation
See 'dolomite'.

Downthrown
See 'fault'.

Drift
Unconsolidated material deposited by ice or by glacial meltwater. Compare with 'Solid'*. With reference to geological maps see 'Equipment, Maps and Access', p.1.

Dry valleys
Valleys with no stream at the surface. In most cases dry valleys are found in limestone areas where the drainage is now underground. These valleys were mostly formed during the Pleistocene* when underground water remained frozen but surface meltwater was periodically produced in large volumes to erode the valleys.

Elaterite
A viscous hydrocarbon. Occurs at Windy Knoll (Walk 2).

Erratics
Rocks and boulders found in boulder clay and which differ in rock type from the rocks generally present in the area. **Indicator erratics** have a distinctive rock type that allows their provenance to be identified.

Escape shafts
Structures formed in sediments by the upward 'escape' of animals under threat of being buried during times of rapid sedimentation, see Figs. 64, 65.

Escarpments
Edges produced by the outcrop of tilted tough beds of sedimentary rock, such as sandstones. See Fig. 47.

Extinction event
A time when different groups of organisms became extinct.

Facies ('Fa-sees')
A term indicating the sum of the characteristics of a rock and relating to the conditions of formation of the rock.

Faults
Major fractures in rocks where differential movement is indicated between the opposite sides of the fault. In some cases the displacement is vertical, to produce upthrown and downthrown sides to the fault. In other cases the movement can be horizontal, producing a side-slip fault. Combinations of vertical and horizontal movement can occur. See Figs. 60, 67, 73.

Fault blocks
Ground between faults.

Feldspar
An important group of rock-forming minerals, comprising about 60 per cent of the Earth's crust. The feldspars are aluminium silicates with a range of composition involving potassium, sodium and calcium. They exhibit good mineral cleavage*.

Fluorite (fluorspar)
A mineral, calcium fluoride, CaF_2. Various uses, e.g., as a flux in melting; in the manufacture of chlorofluorocarbons (CFCs) and the hydrochlorofluorocarbons which are replacing the CFCs.

Fossil
The remains or impressions of organisms preserved from the prehistoric past.

Frame saw
Rock saw for cutting blocks of rock (usually sandstone) into slabs a few centimetres thick for paving and other purposes. The rough surfaces generated on the sawn faces are frequently seen on sandstone flags, see Fig. 12a. An example of a frame saw is seen on Walk 15.

Galena
The most important ore mineral of lead, lead sulphide, PbS. Very dense, with a bright metallic lustre when fresh.

Ganister
A variety of seatearth* (fossil soil), but where the grains and cement are both composed of silica.

Gastropods
The group of molluscs to which the snails belong. They have a long

geological history, ranging from the Cambrian (see Fig. 2) to the present.

Geopetal infill
Partial infilling of sediment in a rock or fossil cavity. This infill serves as a spirit level and can be used to establish the plane of the horizontal at the time of sedimentation. See Fig. 7.

Goniatites
Extinct group of coiled shells belonging to the molluscs. These shells underwent rapid evolution during the Carboniferous so are of great value in (relative*) dating of these rocks.

Granite
An igneous rock*, coarse-grained, with quartz*, feldspar* and mica* grains. Light in colour.

Grit
Term used for coarse-grained sandstone. The term 'Millstone Grit' has been used for that part of the Upper Carboniferous rock succession rich in coarse-grained sandstones, and from which the material was quarried for the manufacture of millstones.

Grikes
See 'clints'*.

Hydrothermal
Term applied to hot water or brines at depth where solution of metals (such as lead or copper) takes place. Once in solution these metals are brought to higher levels by convection flow and precipitated into cavities along fault fracture zones, etc.

Incised
A term used to describe a deeply entrenched valley. Incised streams indicate a time of accelerated erosion.

Igneous ('Fire') Rocks.
One of the three major groups of rocks. Igneous rocks mostly have an origin as molten rock (magma).

Impermeable
Will not allow the passage of fluids such as water.

Inlier
An outcrop of rocks older than the rocks in the surrounding area. A window through younger rocks into the older rocks beneath. See 'Outlier'*.

Interglacial
Interval of warmer climate separating periods of glaciation.

Joints

Systems of fractures more or less at right angles to the bedding in sedimentary rocks. Distinguished from faults by the absence of displacement. Joints disappear at depth and appear to be caused by progressive relief of overburden load as erosion proceeds at the surface. See Fig. 5.

Jurassic

A geological Period of time, and System of rocks, dating from 213 to 144 million years ago. See Fig. 2.

Kaolin

China Clay. A group of clay minerals, the best known of which is kaolinite. The clay minerals are formed by chemical breakdown of such rock-forming minerals as the feldspars. Hydrous aluminium silicates.

Karst

Type of scenery developed in limestone areas due to surface and subsurface solution. Characteristic features include clints*, grikes*, caves.

Knoll Reefs

Masses of limestone which formed as mounds on the sea floor. They were bound by a calcareous cement in some way, little understood, but probably involving bacterial action. Lacking an organic binding skeletal structure they are not directly comparable with modern reefs, but probably formed in similar environments.

Lamination

Presence of thin bands of sedimentary rock, less than 1mm in thickness.

Landslip

Rapid mass movement of rocks and soil downslope, by gravity.

Law of Superposition

In undeformed strata the higher beds are younger than the lower.

Limestone

A sedimentary rock composed essentially of the mineral calcite*.

Magnesian Limestone

A limestone of Permian* age, with the mineral dolomite* present in addition to calcite.

Magnetic dip

The inclination from the horizontal of the Earth's magnetic lines of force.

Magnetic polarity reverses
The polarity of the Earth's magnetic field is known to reverse periodically. The interval between reversals is variable.

Malachite
A copper ore mineral, $Cu_2(CO_3)(OH)_2$. Typically found in the weathering zone of other copper ore minerals.

Marble
As a geological term, 'marble' is limestone that has been recrystallised by heat and/or pressure. As a mason's term, 'marble' is any soft rock that takes a good polish. Beware!

Marine band
A band of rock up to a few metres in thickness, usually composed of clayrock or siltstone, with marine fossils. Marine bands occur in the Upper Carboniferous rocks of the Peak District, and indicate marine incursions into the delta area at the time of deposition.

Mica
A group of rock-forming minerals, characterised by one perfect mineral cleavage*, resulting in a flaky nature, in consequence of the atomic structure. They are aluminium silicates, with a range of compositions including potassium (in the white micas) and iron/magnesium (in the black micas).

Milankovitch Cycles
Climatic cycles resulting from cyclic variation in the form of the Earth's orbit round the Sun, together with cyclic changes in the attitude of the Earth's rotational axis. Such cycles are responsible for the alternation of Glacial and Interglacial phases during the Pleistocene* glaciation.

Millstone Grit Series
The lower part of the Upper Carboniferous succession in the north of England. This succession contains important, thick, coarse-grained sandstones ('gritstones') which were the source material for the manufacture of millstones. However, the term Millstone Grit Series has now largely been replaced by 'Namurian'*. See Fig. 2.

Mineral
Naturally occurring, non-biological, substance with a specific chemical composition (or specific range of chemical compositions) and atomic structure.

Mineralisation
The process by which mineral deposits are formed.

Mineral cleavage
Planes of weakness in minerals, a consequence of the atomic structure of the mineral.

Miocene
An interval of geological time dating from 25 million years ago to 5 million years ago. See Fig. 2.

Moulds
Impressions of fossils or other objects in rocks.

Mudflake conglomerates
Sedimentary rocks containing pebbles of clayrock or siltstone.

'Mussels'
A group of molluscs, with two valves (see Fig. 65) which are mirror-images of one another (unlike the valves of brachiopods) and which are common, as fossils, in the Upper Carboniferous. They appear to have lived in lakes and lagoons.

Namurian
Name of the geological time period (Age) and rock succession (Stage) dating from 320 to 315 million years ago, in the late Carboniferous. An international term. Corresponds to the Millstone Grit Series of the Peak District. See Fig. 2.

Neptunian Dykes
Ancient sediment-infilled fissures within a rock. Most dykes consist of intrusions of igneous rock into fissures that cut across other rocks.

New Red Sandstones
Succession of conglomerates*, sandstones*, and clayrocks* dominantly red in colour, and of Permo-Triassic* age. These rocks formed under arid, desert conditions.

'Oil test'
Films of what appear to be oil on water can be tested by touching with a stick or similar object. If the film re-unites on removal of the stick, then the material is oil. If, however, the film separates into separate 'rafts' then the material is a film of iron oxide – iron hydroxide.

Oolitic
A type of limestone which is composed of calcite spheres, each usually less than 1 mm in diameter. These spheres resemble fish eggs, hence the term 'oolitic'.

Outlier
An outcrop of rocks younger than the rocks in the surrounding

area. A remnant of a rock formation isolated by erosion. See 'Inlier'*.

Palaeomagnetism
The magnetic field in past geological times. The magnetic properties of rocks relating to the magnetic field at the time of their formation is known as the Remanent Magnetism.

Pangaea
The supercontinent comprised of all the major continental areas of Earth, formed at the end of the Carboniferous, then began to break up during the Permo-Triassic*, first into two continents, Laurasia in the north and Gondwanaland in the south. Further break up has produced the continents of today.

Parting lineation
Bedding surface feature of thinly-bedded sandstones caused by alignment of sediment grains by current flow. See Fig. 12b.

Permian
A period of Geological time or System of rocks dating from 286 to 248 million years. See Fig.2.

Permeable
Permits the passage of fluids such as water.

Permo-Triassic
The combined Permian and Triassic Periods of geological time and Systems of rocks dating from 286 to 213 million years ago.

Pillar and stall
Technique of mining in more or less horizontal beds of coal, ore, etc. Extraction is carried out in 'stalls' or headings, whilst roof support is maintained by pillars of the coal or ore and, in some cases, of stonework.

Plate Tectonics
The concept whereby the Earth's crust consists of a number of separate pieces (Plates) which can move relative to one another because of flow in the mantle beneath.

Pleistocene
An Epoch of geological time or Series of rocks dating from 2 million years ago to 10,000 years ago. See Fig. 2.

Pleistocene Glaciation (Ice Age)
A major Glaciation, comprising a number of glacial and interglacial intervals.

Pliocene
An Epoch of geological time or Series of rocks dating from 5 to 2 million years ago. See Fig.2.

Plug and feather
A combination of a chisel or wedge ('plug') and two flanking sleeves ('feathers'). Sets of plugs and feathers are inserted into a line of short bored holes and knocked in, progressively, to break the stone along a more or less straight line. See Fig. 56.

Plunge
The inclination from the horizontal of a rock fold and the compass direction of the fold axis.

Productoid brachiopods
A group of brachiopods in which the two valves have the same convexity, very common in the Carboniferous. In life both valves were concave-up.

Pyrite or Fool's Gold.
A common mineral, iron sulphide, FeS_2. Its colour looks like gold! But it is brittle not malleable.

Quartz
A common rock-forming mineral, silica, silicon dioxide, SiO_2. Glassy, hard.

Quaternary
The Pleistocene and Holocene combined. The last 2 million years of geological time, see Fig. 2.

Radiometric dating
The technique of dating by use of radioactive elements in minerals and rocks. Age can be calculated by reference to the ratio in amounts between parent radioactive substance and daughter products.

Rake
Derbyshire term for 'mineral vein'.

Reddened
Term applied to the weathered zone often present in the Carboniferous rocks immediately below the contact with overlying rocks of Permo-Triassic age. Due to arid weathering of the Carboniferous surface prior to burial beneath Permo-Triassic sediments.

Refractory
Able to withstand high temperatures, for example, material suitable for use as furnace linings.

Relative age
Ages relative to the ages of other rocks, etc. Some events or rocks, are younger or older than others. Contrast with Absolute Age*.

Remanent magnetism
The magnetic properties of rocks relating to the magnetic field at the time of their formation.

Ripple marks
Structures formed in sand or silt by flowing or oscillating water and which are often preserved in ancient sediments, see Fig. 12d.

Ripple lamination
Cross section revealing the detailed internal structure of the sediment in fossil ripple marks. See lamination*.

Sandstone
Sedimentary rock composed of sand, compacted and bound by a natural cement.

Saw marks
Features seen on sandstone paving flags where surfaces are scratched and scored by the action of frame saws*, see Fig. 12a. A frame saw can be seen in a display of quarry machinery at Tegg's Nose (Walk 15).

Scarp slope
Steep hillside developed along the outcrop of a tough rock layer or stratum. Scarp slopes should be distinguished from dip slopes*, see Fig. 42

Seatearth
A fossil soil horizon. Distinguished by the presence of fossil roots. When the seatearth is siliceous in nature it is known as ganister*. Where the seatearth is suitable for making refractory* products, like firebricks, it is known as fireclay. See Figs. 4a, b.

Sedimentary Rocks
One of the three major groups of rocks. They were formed as sediments accumulated in a variety of environments, then buried, compacted and cemented.

Setts
Natural stone, brick-shaped, paving blocks.

Shale
A term formerly used for 'clayrock'*.

Shelf facies
Rocks, the characteristics of which ('facies'*) indicate deposition on the floor of a shallow shelf sea.

Siderite
An ore mineral, iron carbonate, $FeCO_3$. Occurs as the cement in some concretions*.

Silicification
The introduction of silica into rocks and fossils, involving replacement of original material such as calcite.

Siltstone
Sedimentary rock composed predominantly of silt-sized grains. These grains are often not large enough to be seen easily, but can be detected by a distinct grittiness on the teeth when bitten (a test not recommended!).

Sill
A body of igneous* rock which forms a sheet parallel to the bedding of associated sedimentary rocks.

Slate
A metamorphic rock, where fine-grained rock (sedimentary or volcanic, usually) is subject to intense compression to produce natural planes of weakness at right angles to the pressure. These planes of weakness are known as rock cleavage, which should be distinguished from mineral cleavage*.

Slickensides
The scored and polished surfaces formed by movements on faults. See Fig. 67.

Slump structures
Deformation structures produced by sediment movement (usually by gravity) during the time of sediment deposition.

Soil creep
Progressive movement downslope of soil by gravity.

'Solid'
Reference to the consolidated rock materials of an area as distinct from the unconsolidated deposits of sand, gravel, etc. Contrast with 'Drift'*. With reference to geological maps see 'Equipment, Maps and Access'.

Sough
Mine drainage tunnel. Pronounced "suff".

Sphalerite
An important zinc ore mineral, zinc sulphide, ZnS.

Spheroidal weathering
Chemical weathering that has progressed along joints and fractures, isolating relatively fresh cores of rock, which are essentially spherical in form. Especially characteristic of basalt* and dolerite*.

Spring line
Line of springs on a hillside indicating the level at which permeable rocks (above) meet impermeable rocks (below). See Fig. 47.

Stacking
The locking together of curved shells (including fossil shells) in the manner of a stack of saucers. Indicative of turbulent conditions. See Fig. 58.

Stalactites
Elongate candle-like deposits of precipitated calcite which hang down from cave roofs.

Stalagmites
Mounds of precipitated calcite built up on the floors of caves.

Stratification
The layering in beds of sedimentary rock. See Fig. 5.

Stromatolites
Banded structures in limestone, formed by the action of Cyanobacteria*. See Fig. 37.

Syncline
Downfold in sedimentary strata, where the youngest rocks form the core of the structure. An example is the Goyt Syncline, see Fig. 6a and 72. See 'anticlines'.

Terminal curvature
Strata at outcrop on hillsides pulled over by soil creep above, see Fig. 49.

Terracettes
Small terraces developed on steep hillsides, each a minute landslip, indicating soil instability. See Fig. 62.

Tertiary
The Period of geological time or System of rocks dating from 65 to 2 million years ago. See Fig. 2.

Tors
Upstanding masses of rock which appear to be rather tougher than

the surrounding rocks, possibly because of different cementation and/or fewer joints.

U-shaped Valley

A valley which has either been glaciated at some time, or which has acquired its form by landsliding of the valley sides. See Fig.13.

Upthrown

See 'fault'.

Vesicle

A cavity such as a gas bubble. Note the adjective 'Vesicular'.

Volcanic vents

Masses of volcanic rock representing the remains of the lava-filled pipe of a former volcano.

Weathering

The processes of surface chemical and physical change which occur on the Earth's surface.

Westphalian

A European term for the geological time period (Age) and rock succession (Stage) dating from 315 to 296 million years ago, in the late Carboniferous. Corresponds approximately to the 'Coal Measures' of the Peak District. See Fig. 2.

Further Information

Books

There are many good introductory books to geology, but a particularly good one is: *Earth Story*, by Simon Lamb and David Singleton, published by the BBC.

There is a wide range of colour guides to rocks, minerals and fossils available. In general they are all good, and their inspection is recommended. They are available in all good bookshops.

A dictionary of geology is always useful. Again there is a choice of paperback dictionaries, all good, available from most bookshops.

There are a number of geological guides, written primarily for amateur and professional geologists rather than for the rambler. The best known of these are published by the Geologists' Association and include Guide No. 26 *The Peak District* by F. Wolverson Cope, and No. 56, *The Castleton Area, Derbyshire,* by Trevor D. Ford. Copies of these guides are available in the Peak Park centres and can also be obtained from the Geologists' Association, Burlington House, Piccadilly, London W1V 9AG, telephone 020 7434 9298.

Attention was drawn in the description to Walk 14 to the guide *Lead Mining in the Peak District*, edited by T.D. Ford and J. H. Rieuwerts and published by Landmark Publishing Ltd. This book is generally available at various outlets in the Peak District.

Maps

The **Ordnance Survey** topographical maps (one covering the entire district at the scale of 1:63 360, others at the scales of 1:50 000 and 1:25 000) are readily available from bookshops, from Peak Park offices and other outlets. Enquiries should be made to the Ordnance Survey at Explorer House, Adanac Drive, Southampton, SO16 0AS telephone08456 050505 or go to the web site: www,ordnancesurvey.co.uk

A special Holiday Geology Map for the Peak District has been published by the **British Geological Survey,** and is available at Peak Park centres. This map and other, more detailed, geological maps of the Peak District (see Walk descriptions for details of maps available) are available from the British Geological Survey, Kingsley Dunham Centre, Keyworth, Nottingham NG12 5GG, telephone 0115 936 3103 (3241 for Sales Desk), website: www.bgs.ac.uk

Equipment

Hand lenses (recommended magnification x10), and other equipment useful in field work, are available from Geo Supplies Ltd., 49 Station Road, Chapeltown, Sheffield S35 2XE, telephone 0114 245 5746, www.geosupplies.co.uk. Geo Supplies also carry stocks of geological maps and books.

Also from Sigma Leisure:

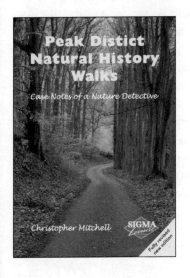

Peak District Walking Natural History Walks
Christopher Mitchell

An updated 2nd Edition with 18 varied walks for all lovers of the great outdoors — and armchair ramblers too! Learn how to be a nature detective, a 'case notes' approach shows you what clues to look for and how to solve them. Detailed maps include animal tracks and signs, landscape features and everything you need for the perfect natural history walk. There are mysteries and puzzles to solve to add more fun for family walks — solutions supplied! Includes follow on material with an extensive Bibliography and 'Taking it Further' sections. *£8.99*

Dark Peak Hikes
Off the Beaten Track
Doug Brown

Here are 30 walks in the Dark Peak - the legendary northern part of the Peak District that covers some of the best hill country of Derbyshire, Yorkshire and Greater Manchester. Renowned for its unique peat ecology and striking gritstone scenery, the Dark Peak is a paradise for adventurous walkers intent on exploring the remoter parts of the moors.

Includes lots of helpful information for each walk – starting point, distance and estimated time, a general description including level of difficulty, and a very detailed route description. *£8.99*

Peak District Walks
starting from train stations
Peter Naldrett

Two types of train station walks are covered in this book: there are those from existing train stations that still have passengers bustling about them, and there are those from platforms that fell silent in the infamous closures of the 1960s. Whether you are wanting to reach your starting point via train or delve into the history of transport in the Peak District, this book has something for you. One thing all the train station walks have in common is that they enjoy a fabulous route into some breath-taking countryside. Gorges, woodland, moors, farmland, rivers, glacial valleys and some tremendous hills are all included in this series of 20 walks, linked together by the transport routes that, today and in the past, dissected the Peak District.
£8.99

High Pub Walks
In the Peak District
Martin Smith

The Peak District National Park is noted for more than just its scenery. It also has a wealth of real ale pubs, many of which lie above 1000 feet (304 metres). It's these pubs that feature in this book. What better way to visit them than on foot? The book describes 30 walks and also has lots of information about the areas through which the various routes pass. The walks vary in length from a mere 2½ miles to 12¾ miles, so there's something suitable for everyone here. The walks generally start from the pub and with certain rare exceptions, can be reached by public transport, so you can leave your car at home and savour the liquid products on offer.
£8.99

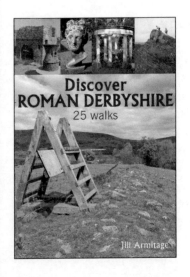

Discover Roman Derbyshire
25 walks
Jill Armitage

The Romans have been credited with giving Britain a network of roads that still has a profound effect on our road systems, so Discover Roman Derbyshire, 25 walks sets out to trace those roads on foot in the same manner that the Roman soldiers did when they occupied the region between the 1st and 5th centuries. The roads linked forts with their accompanying vici, busy trading centres where industry prospered similar to our present day towns. The walks not only include the roads, forts and vici, they also trace localities where finds have been discovered.

£8.99

Discover Celtic Derbyshire
25 walks
Jill Armitage

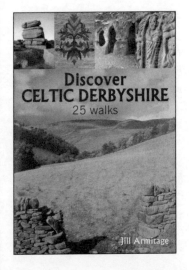

Discover Celtic Derbyshire follows the Portway from the key Celtic Hillfort of Mam Tor in North Derbyshire to the Derbyshire/Nottinghamshire border at Stapleford and the southern river ports. Along the route, you will encounter the hermitages and industries, visit tribal hillforts, those iconic symbols of the age, and through megalithic mysteries, ancient feasts and festivals, discover the lifestyle of these people the conquering Romans considered barbaric. They were not. They had their beliefs and their gods and the Roman conquest of Britain did not signal the immediate death of Celtic culture. That is why this area has a treasure trove of early curiosities and customs, showing that pre-history is not quite dead in this ancient heart of England. Of the 25 walks in this book, 15 are circular, however, the route of the ancient Portway has been divided into ten manageable walks ranging from 3½ -7 miles.

£8.99

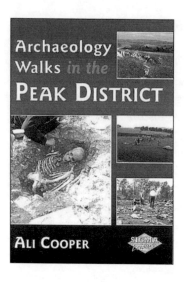

Archaeology Walks in The Peak District
Ali Cooper

These walks explore archaeological sites where there are visible pre-historic features in the landscape: Bronze age barrows, stone circles, caves, mines and much more. Walks are from 3 to 12 miles and are fully illustrated. The book includes an introduction to the study of archaeology and a glossary of the terminology used. Brief descriptions of the major finds on the walks are included, plus a bibliography for those who wish to delve deeper. Ali Cooper has an MA in archaeology and is a keen outdoors enthusiast.
£8.99

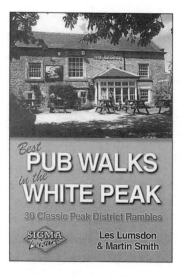

Best Pub Walks in the Dark Peak &
Best Pub Walks in the White Peak
Les Lumsdon and Martin Smith

These two books, both by Les Lumsdon and Martin Smith, provide comprehensive coverage of the entire Peak District. Inspiring walks and welcoming pubs enable walkers to appreciate the history, landscape and personalities of the area. These books were published by us originally in the 1980s and have recently been completely updated to ensure accuracy. Each book costs *£9.99*

Derbyshire Walks with Children
William D Parke

All these walks are less than six miles long, with 'escape routes' for the young or less energetic. *"The needs, entertainment and safety of children have been of paramount importance."*
– Peak Advertiser

£8.99

Peak District Walking – On The Level
Norman Buckley

Some folk prefer easy walks, and sometimes there's just not time for an all-day yomp. In either case, this is definitely a book to keep on your bookshelf. Norman Buckley has had considerable success with "On The Level" books for the Lake District and the Yorkshire Dales.

The walks are ideal for family outings and the precise instructions ensure that there's little chance of losing your way. Well-produced maps encourage everybody to try out the walks - all of which are well scattered across the Peak District.

£8.99

All-Terrain Pushchair Walks: The Peak District
Alison Southern

The Peak District, in the heart of the country, has some of England's most picturesque landscapes, from the White Peak in the south with its rocky outcrops and steep hills, to the Dark Peak in the north with peat moss moorland and stunning vistas. This book is for families with all-terrain pushchairs and buggies, and for everyone wishing to avoid as many stiles and obstacles as possible. Includes family-friendly attractions, trees to identify, birds and plants to spot, and lots more to discover. Have fun while you walk enjoying the amazing views, have some healthy exercise and spend time with the family away from the modern world.

£8.99

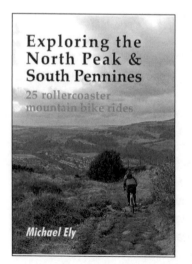

Exploring the North Peak & South Pennines
25 rollercoaster mountain bike rides
Michael Ely

This book will inspire you to pump up the tyres and oil the chain for some excitement, exercise and a feast of rollercoaster riding as you join Michael Ely on some great mountain biking in these Pennine hills. Over 500 miles of riding for the adventurous off-road cyclist that explore the tracks and steep lanes in the Pennine hills. There are twenty-five illustrated rides - with cafe stops half way round - to provide both a challenge and many hours of healthy exercise in classic mountain biking country.

£8.99

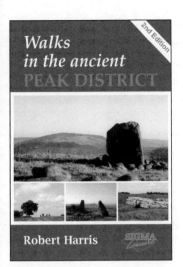

Walks in the Ancient Peak District
Robert Harris

A collection of walks visiting the prehistoric monuments and sites of the Peak District. A refreshing insight into the thinking behind the monuments, the rituals and strange behaviour of our ancestors. All the routes are circular, most starting and finishing in a town or village that is easy to locate and convenient to reach by car.

£8.99

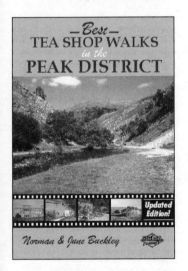

Best Tea Shop Walks in the Peak District
Norman and June Buckley

A wonderful collection of easy-going walks that are ideal for families and all those who appreciate fine scenery with a touch of decadence in the shape of an afternoon tea or morning coffee —or both! The 26 walks are spread widely across the Peak District, including Lyme Park, Castleton, Miller's Dale, and The Roaches and — of course — such famous dales as Lathkill and Dovedale. Each walk has a handy summary so that you can choose the walks that are ideally suited to the interests and abilities of your party. The tea shops are just as diverse, ranging from the splendour of Chatsworth House to more basic locations. Each one welcomes ramblers and there is always a good choice of tempting goodies.

£8.99

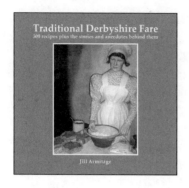
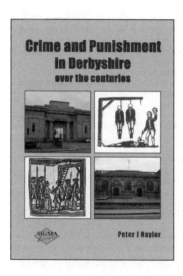